Provence
&
The Côte d'Azur

by Teresa Fisher

Teresa Fisher is a confirmed Francophile and
experienced travel writer who has written or
contributed to numerous guides on holiday
destinations throughout Europe including the AA
publications *Village France*, *Journey Through
France*, *Essential French Riviera*, and *Spiral Guide
to Paris*.

D0258411

Written by Teresa Fisher

First published 1998
Reprinted 2002. Information verified and updated
Reprinted Oct 2002. Reprinted Jan 2004, May
2004
**This edition 2005. Information verified and
updated.**

© Automobile Association Developments
Limited 1998, 2002, 2005

*The pace of life in
Provence is relaxed*

Published by AA Publishing, a trading name of Automobile
Association Developments Limited, whose registered
office is Southwood East, Apollo Rise, Farnborough,
Hampshire, GU14 0JW. Registered number 1878835.

A CIP catalogue record for this book is available from the
British Library.

The contents of this publication are believed correct at
the time of printing. Nevertheless, the publishers cannot be
held responsible for any errors or omissions or for changes
in the details given in this guide or for the consequences of
any reliance on the information it provides. This does not
affect your statutory rights. Assessments of attractions,
hotels, restaurants and other sights are based upon the
author's personal experience and, therefore, necessarily
contain elements of subjective opinion which may not
reflect the publisher's opinion or dictate a reader's own
experience on another occasion. We have tried to ensure
accuracy in this guide, but things do change and we would
be grateful if readers would advise us of any inaccuracies
they may encounter.

Find out more about
AA Publishing and the
wide range of travel
publications and services
the AA provides by
visiting our website at
www.theAA.com/bookshop

A01990

Colour separation: BTB, Digital Imaging, Whitchurch,
Hampshire
Printed and bound in Italy by Printer Trento Srl

Contents

About this Book 4

About this Book

KEY TO SYMBOLS

✚ map reference to the maps found in the What to See section (see below)

✉ address or location

☎ telephone number

🕐 opening times

🍴 restaurant or café on premises or near by

Ⓜ nearest underground train station

🚌 nearest bus/tram route

🚃 nearest overground train station

🛳 ferry crossings and excursions by boat

✈ travel by air

ℹ tourist information

♿ facilities for visitors with disabilities

✋ admission charge

↔ other places of interest near by

❓ other practical information

► indicates the page where you will find a fuller description

---

This book is divided into five sections to cover the most important aspects of your visit to Provence.

Viewing Provence pages 5–14
An introduction to Provence & The Côte d'Azur by the author.
Features of Provence & The Côte d'Azur
Essence of Provence & The Côte d'Azur
The Shaping of Provence & The Côte d'Azur
Peace and Quiet
Famous of Provence & The Côte d'Azur

Top Ten pages 15–26
The author's choice of the Top Ten places to visit in Provence & The Côte d'Azur, each with practical information.

What to See pages 27–90
The four main areas of Provence & The Côte d'Azur, each with its own brief introduction and an alphabetical listing of the main attractions within the area.
Practical information
Snippets of 'Did you know…' information
3 suggested walks
2 suggested tours
2 features

Where To... pages 91–116
Detailed listings of the best places to eat, stay, shop, take the children and be entertained.

Practical Matters pages 117–24
A highly visual section containing essential travel information.

Maps
All map references are to the individual maps found in the What to See section of this guide. For example, St-Tropez has the reference ✚ 69C1 – indicating the page on which the map is located and the grid square in which St-Tropez is to be found. The maps used can be found in the index.

Prices
Where appropriate, an indication of the cost of an establishment is given by € signs: €€€ denotes higher prices, €€ denotes average prices, while € denotes lower charges.

Star Ratings
Most of the places described in this book have been given a separate rating:
✪✪✪   Do not miss
✪✪   Highly recommended
✪   Worth seeing

Viewing
Provence

Above: *commercial lavender growing*
Right: *changing the guard in Monaco*

5

Teresa Fisher's Provence & The Côte d'Azur

It looked astonishingly beautiful in Maurice Pagnol's films *Jean de Florette* and *Manon des Source*, and Peter Mayle's celebrated books present life there as an idyll, but what is Provence really like?

Is it the untamed marshes of the Camargue; or the snow-clad mountains of the Alps; or perhaps the shimmering heat of the beautiful beaches and the exotic palms of the chic resorts which line the Mediterranean coastline?

Most visitors are at a loss to know where to start, such is the variety of the landscape and the wealth of ancient history. But for many the true essence of Provence can be found in the myriad sleepy medieval villages, precariously perched on steep hillsides or hidden in a sun-drenched landscape of silvery olive groves, vineyards and parasol pines, splashed with poppy fields and scented stripes of lavender, stretching like mauve corduroy across the countryside, the air heavy with all the perfumes of Provence, and the countryside painted with the vivid palette of van Gogh and Cézanne.

No wonder Provence and the Côte d'Azur is France's most visited region, with its exceptional cultural heritage, and its rich diversity of landscape, cuisine, climate and peoples. Yet despite its popularity it is still possible to escape the tourist hordes and discover your own hidden delights – tiny sun-kissed vineyards and secret sun-baked coves; bustling markets; romantic châteaux or a dusty game of boules; coffee and croissants in a village café, pastis in the bar...

New visitors soon fall under the region's spell. Those who already know it remain enchanted, returning year after year for a taste of *la vie Provençale*.

Defining the Boundaries

The regions of Provence and the Côte d'Azur are difficult to define as, since the Roman Provincia of 125 BC, Provence's borders have moved countless times. Today it comprises the region Provence-Alpes-Côte-d'Azur, made up of the *départements*: Alpes-Maritimes, Bouches-du-Rhône, Alpes-de-Haute-Provence, Hautes-Alpes, Var and Vaucluse. Officially the Côte d'Azur stretches from the French-Italian frontier to St-Raphaël, although the expression is frequently applied to the whole French Riviera as far as Marseille.

Features of Provence & The Côte d'Azur

Geography
- One of 22 regions of France
- *Départements:* Alpes-Maritimes, Alpes-de-Haute-Provence, Bouches-du-Rhône, Hautes-Alpes, Vaucluse and Var.
- Surface area: 31,436sq km (Monaco: 2sq km)
- Protected monuments and buildings: 1,500
- Highest mountain: La Meije (3,983m)

People
- Inhabitants: 4.5 million (including 375,000 foreigners); 90% live in large cities and their suburbs.
- People with second homes here: 400,000
- Largest city: Marseille (population: 1.2 million)
- Annual visitors to coast: 8 million
- Tourist revenue: €7 billion

Climate
- Average annual temperature range: -1°C–22°C (mountains); 6°C–24°C (coast)
- Sea temperature range: 10°–25°C
- Annual hours of sunshine: 3,000 (over 300 days a year)
- Annual rainfall: 550–820mm (Nov and Mar are wettest)
- Mistral wind: up to 290kph; 100–150 days a year

Agriculture & Industry
- Percentage of France's total production: lemons (70%); cut flowers (50%); fruit and vegetables (20%); rice (25%); melons (30%); olives (52%); grapes (50%)
- Flowers produced: 172 million roses; 188 million carnations
- Percentage of world production: lavender oil (70%)
- Farmers: 20,000
- 1,500 fishermen catch 20,000 tonnes (including 10,000 tonnes of sardines!)

Wine
- Classified wine regions: 18
- *Appellation d'origine contrôlée* (AOC) wines: 8
- Vineyards: 16 per cent of region's agricultural land; 11 per cent of France's vineyards
- Average size of vineyard: 6 hectares
- People employed by the wine trade: 20,000

Economy
Provence and the Côte d'Azur is vital to France's economy, mainly due to Marseille, the country's second city and one of the world's leading ports. Ninety per cent of Marseille's imports is oil and the massive surrounding industrial area produces 85 per cent of France's aluminium and 30 per cent of its natural gas. Tourism plays a major role, along with research and high-tech industries, notably the Nice-Sophia-Antipolis technology park, France's 'Silicon Valley'.

Facing page: *a taste of Provence – cobbled stones, golden sunlight and sleepy mountaintop villages*

Below: *a market trader sells his burnished sweet chestnuts*

Essence of Provence & The Côte d'Azur

The many facets and charms of Provence and the Côte d'Azur are impossible to chart, so varied are they, making choices almost impossible. Should you pack your paintbox, walking boots, swimsuit, skis or all of them? One suggestion is that on your first visit concentrate solely on the ambience – the brilliant sunshine, the sparkling air, the superb food, the unforgettable scenery and the friendly locals – for it is certain you will become a devotee and return again and again to experience what the addicted already know but would rather keep to themselves!

Street artists in Avignon capture the essence of Provence on canvas

THE **10** ESSENTIALS

*If you only have a short time to visit Provence,
or would like to get a really complete picture of the
region, here are the essentials:*

*Relax by the waterfront or
on a shady terrace*

• **Soak up the sun on one
of the Riviera's sandy
beaches,** or relax under the
shade of a classic striped
parasol.

• **Visit a perfumery in
Grasse,** and create your very
own Provençal scent (➤ 88).

• **Taste some of the
world's finest wines** at
Châteauneuf-du-Pape.

• **Taste *la vraie*
bouillabaisse** in Marseille,
near the old port where the
dish originated.

• **Spot the rich and famous
at the Cannes Film Festival,**
the glitziest, most glamorous
event of them all.

• **Try your hand at
gambling** in Monte-Carlo's
world-famous casino.

• **Don your diamonds and
the latest in haute couture
and promenade the
waterfront at St-Tropez,**
admiring its ostentatious
yachts and gin palaces.

• **Splash through the
marshes of the Camargue**
on horseback, accompanied
by local *gardian* cowboys
(➤ 17).

• **Go shopping in a bright,
bustling village market,**
and treat yourself to a
relaxing picnic of goodies –

goat's cheese,
tomatoes, olives
and wine – in the
sleepy surrounding
countryside.

• **Join locals in a
game of boules** –
this ancient game
originated here
and, although it is
now played all
round the world,
the most fiercely
contested games
still take place in
the shady squares
of Provence.

*The mountain
village of Gourdon
has an amazing
view of the Loup
river*

The Shaping of Provence & The Côte d'Azur

c900,000 BC
First signs of human settlement.

c3,500 BC
First *borie* villages (► 19).

c600 BC
Greeks found port of Massalia (Marseille) and introduce olives, vines and ceramics.

300 BC
Celtic invasions of Provence.

218 BC
Hannibal crosses region to reach Italy.

125 BC
Romans conquer southern Gaul and name it Provincia.

58–52 BC
Caesar's conquest of Gaul.

3rd–5th Century AD
Spread of Christianity.

395
Arles becomes administrative capital of Roman Gaul.

476
Fall of Roman Empire.

536
Provence comes under Frankish rule.

8–10th Century
Saracens invade southern France; Provence becomes part of the Carolingian empire.

855
Kingdom of Provence created for Charlemagne's grandson, Charles the Bald.

1032
Provence becomes part of Holy Roman Empire.

12–14th Century
Troubadour poetry and courtly love flourishes (► 47).

1266
Charles I of Anjou, (already duke of Provence) is crowned king of Provence.

1308
The Genoese Grimaldi family purchase the estate of Monaco.

1309
Frenchman, Clement V, becomes Pope; Papacy established in Avignon until 1376.

1409
Aix University is founded.

1481
Death of Good King René, last count of Provence (► 52). Region falls to France.

1501
Provençal parliament founded in Aix.

1535
Nostradamus born at St-Rémy.

1539
French replaces Provençal, the *langue d'oc*, as official language.

1559
Town and duchy of Orange fall to William of Nassau, prince of Orange.

1691
Nice occupied by the French, but returned to Savoy in 1696.

1720
Plague kills over 100,000 people.

1789
French Revolution, Republicans adopt army song *La Marseillaise* (► 55).

1791
France annexes Avignon and the Comtat Venaissin.

1814
Napoléon lands in Provence.

1830
Provençal poet laureate Frédéric Mistral is born at Maillane.

1830s
Beginnings of tourism on the French Riviera.

1839
Artist Paul Cézanne born

at Aix-en-Provence.

1854
Foundation of the Félibrige literary circle with the aim of promoting the Provençal language.

1855
Paris and Avignon linked by rail.

1860
Nice votes to join France.

1866
Monte-Carlo founded; casino opened in 1878.

1888
Van Gogh moves to Arles from Paris.

1920s–30s
Côte d'Azur becomes a fashionable summer resort.

1928
Camargue National Park created.

1933
Waters of the Rhône first harnessed for energy.

1942
Nazis invade southern France.

1944
Allied troops land on the Côte d'Azur.

1946
Picasso moves to Antibes.

1947
First Cannes Film Festival.

1956
Monaco's Prince Rainer III marries Grace Kelly.

1959
Floods in Fréjus kill 421.

1962
Algerian war of independence; many French North Africans settle in Provence.

1968
Marseille harbour becomes too small for rapid industrial growth; Étang de Berre industrial harbour opened.

1970
Autoroute du Soleil completed.

1972
Regionalisation of French *départements;* five form the region Provence-Alpes-Côte-d'Azur.

1981
Paris and Marseille linked by TGV.

1980s
Extreme-right political parties gain popularity in key Provençal cities.

1992
Freak floods devastate parts of the Vaucluse and claim lives in Vaison-la-Romaine.

2002
The euro becomes France's official currency.

752. - MONTE-CARLO. - Place du Casino - Café de Paris
Casino Place - Coffee-house

Monte-Carlo's heyday

11

Peace & Quiet

Nature has been infinitely generous with Provence and the Côte d'Azur. You only need to wander through the fields and forests, to hike in the hills, gorges and mountains or to stroll along the shore to discover a vast array of flora and fauna in these varied habitats. It is, without doubt, a naturalist's paradise.

The Coast

With the colourful bird life of the Riviera, in particular the bright yellow serins and Sardinian warblers of the rocky Esterel coast, it is easy to forget that hidden out of sight the Mediterranean supports an abundance of marine creatures. Port-Cros, one of the Îles d'Hyères, and France's only offshore national park, provides a rare opportunity to see the region's rich underwater life. Armed with a mask and flippers, and following a unique underwater path, it is possible to swim with vividly coloured fish (sea peacocks, black-faced blennies), while octopuses and jellyfish lurk among beds of Neptune grass, sponges and sea anemones.

Eagle owls and flamingos – just two of the wonders of the Camargue

Provence's best-known wildlife location and one of Europe's most important wetlands, is the Camargue, famous for its white horses, black bulls, pink flamingos and some of Europe's most exotic birds (➤ 17).

The Hinterland

In the *arrière pays*, northwest of the Camargue, lies the rarely visited plaine de la Crau, a stony plain with sun-bleached scrub and the occasional rock pool, an ideal

habitat for both insects and reptiles. Indeed, five species of non-poisonous snake can be found here, including the rare Montpellier snake. Look out also for pin-tailed sandgrouse, cream-bibbed pratincole and the dazzling orange, yellow, green, blue and black bee-eater, one of Provence's most colourful birds, which feeds on bees and dragonflies, caught on the wing. The low, craggy limestone Alpilles massif beyond attracts birds of prey including Bonelli's eagle, Egyptian vultures and eagle owls.

One of Provence's special delights is to ramble through the region's extensive brushwood habitats (locally called *garrigue*), where the air is fragrant with lavender and the wild herbs – rosemary, thyme, basil, marjoram and tarragon, the delicious *herbes de Provence* – so prominent in regional cuisine.

While its *garrigue* vegetation harbours warblers, hoopoes and blue rock thrushes, the region's sunshine and favourable climate allow many interesting trees to grow, with olive and oak predominant in lower areas, pines, almonds and neat rows of cypresses on the hillsides of the interior, and an abundance of fruit trees. After all, Provence is the market garden of France.

The Mountains

Up in the Hautes-Alpes, the Parc Régional de Queyras is a wild, forgotten corner of the Alps bordering Italy, renowned for its rare wild flowers. To the south, one of France's most beautiful alpine reserves – the Parc National du Mercantour – provides sanctuary for most of Europe's mountain animal species, including wild boar, marmot, chamois, ibex and mouflon (wild sheep) as well as bright butterflies. The sweet, heady perfume of myriad alpine flowers attracts a busy insect life of beetles, bugs and bees – an endless supply of food for the 18 types of bat common to the area.

The snow-capped peaks of the Provençal Alps are never far away

La Pêche

Provence is a paradise for fishermen, with trout, salmon and eel in abundance in the region's countless rivers and lakes. Sea fishing is also popular with well-organised trips from most ports (➤ 115). Look out for a method of fishing unique to the sandy rivers of the Camargue – *pêche à pied* – fishing by foot – where tiny molluscs called *tellines* are gathered by hand, served locally with garlic and parsley as a delicious regional hors d'oeuvre (➤ 37).

Famous of Provence & The Côte d'Azur

Ever since Dijonais vineyard owner Stephen Liegeard visited the Mediterranean in 1887 and exclaimed 'Côte d'Azur!' (thereby christening an already popular winter health resort), a rich assortment of actors, artists, writers and royalty have been attracted to this southern coast of France, from Queen Victoria to Pablo Picasso, and from Frédéric Mistral to Peter Mayle, all seduced by the beauty of its landscapes and the sparkling azure sea. As Nietzche wrote in 1883: 'Here, the days follow on with a beauty that I would describe as almost insolent. I have never lived through a winter of such constant perfection'.

Star Quality
It was not until the 1930s that the Riviera became a summer resort, made fashionable by visiting Americans including Harpo Marx, Isadora Duncan, who met her tragic death here when her scarf became entangled round the axle of her open car, and writer F Scott Fitzgerald. Nowadays the Riviera remains home to Brigitte Bardot, Joan Collins, Elton John, Claudia Schiffer and a whole host of celebrities.

Inspirational Provence
Many writers have been drawn to Provence over the years and it has been the focus of countless literary masterpieces (see panel). However, it is the artists who have left the deepest imprint on the region – Renoir, Dufy, Matisse, Cézanne and van Gogh to name but a few. They have immortalised Provence's most prestigious sites on canvas, having been hypno-tised by the rich palette of landscapes and almost magical, incandescent light, which has provided inspi-ration over centuries – as it does today for a new gener-ation of artists and writers.

*Prince Rainier III of
Monaco with the late
Princess Grace*

Top Ten

Above: *the Calanques near Cassis*
Right: *Giacometti sculpture at the Fondation Maecht*

15

1

The Calanques

✚ 28B1

ℹ Cassis Tourist Office:
quai des Moulins (☎
04 42 01 71 17)

♿ None

✋ Free

↔ Cassis (► 57),
Marseille (► 54)

❓ 45-minute visits by boat
with commentary from
9–6 daily

The most dramatic scenery of the French Riviera – dazzling white cliffs plunging into the sparkling turquoise waters of magnificent mini-fjords.

This fjord-like landscape is unique in Europe. Just outside Cassis, the coast is broken up by a series of tiny, narrow creeks or *calanques*, lying at the foot of sheer limestone cliffs. The vertical, weathered rock faces are popular with climbers and the clear, deep water is ideal for bathing, making the area a popular weekend retreat from nearby Marseille.

The Calanques can only be reached by pleasure cruiser from Cassis or on foot, following a waymarked path across the heather and gorse of the high cliff tops, with a steep scramble down to the beaches. The first and longest *calanque*, Port-Miou, is one of the most picturesque, lined

A stunning view across azure sea to the white rocks of the Calanques

with yachts and pleasure craft. Calanque Port-Pin is the smallest, with a tiny shingle beach shaded by pines (hence the name, although many trees here were destroyed some years ago by a massive forest fire). En Vau, the third inlet, is the most spectacular, with stark precipitous cliffs and needle-like rocks rising from the sea. The 1½-hour walk to reach it, and the ensuing steep descent to the sandy beach keeps it free from crowds.

Further west, the Sormiou and Morgiou creeks can be reached by car. In 1991 French diver Henri Cosquer discovered a Stone Age grotto deep below sea level at Sormiou. It is decorated with ancient paintings of prehistoric animals, similar to those found at Lascaux in the Dordogne. There are doubts about the paintings' authenticity, but, unfortunately, no palaeolithic experts have the ability to dive to 32m in order to decide whether they are genuine.

2
The Camargue

A strange, disparate marshland, renowned for its passionate people, its traditions, its silver-cream horses, black bulls and salmon-pink flamingos.

No area in France matches the Camargue for its landscape: brackish lagoons, flat rice fields and salty marshes, sand spits and coastal dunes, tufted with coarse, spiky grass and interlaced with shallow streams and canals. Even its boundaries – the lesser and greater Rhône deltas and the sea – are forever shifting. This extraordinary landscape harbours an outstanding variety of wildlife and the unique lifestyle of the Camarguais cowboys.

The people of the Camargue are hardy folk. They live in low, thatched, whitewashed cottages with bulls' horns over the door to ward off evil spirits. They proudly guard the Camarguais heritage, by wearing traditional costume and raising horses and cattle on ranches, or *manades*. Contrary to popular belief the famous white horses are not wild. They are actually owned by a *manadier* or breeder, but are left to roam semi-free. Some are also used for trekking expeditions. The small, black local bulls with their distinctive lyre-shaped horns, are bred for the ring (➤ 50). Watching a mounted *gardian* drive his herd through the marshes is a truly unforgettable sight!

The Camargue also offers sanctuary to some of Europe's most exotic water birds, including purple herons and stone curlews. It is the only place in Europe where flamingos breed regularly and in their greatest numbers between April and September. The best months for bird watching are from April to June and September to February.

✚ 28A1

Parc Ornithologique du Pont-du-Gau (Bird Sanctuary)

✉ DN570 from Arles or Stes-Maries-de-la-Mer

☎ 04 90 97 82 62

🕐 Apr–Sep, daily 9 to sunset; Oct–Mar daily 10–5

♿ Few

✋ Expensive

Manade Jacques Bon, Camargue

✉ Le Mas de Peint, 13200 le Sambuc

☎ 04 90 97 20 62

❓ Professional ranch with rodeos and tours on horseback

Musée Camarguais

✉ Mas du Pont de Rousty

☎ 04 90 97 10 82

🕐 Daily 9–6 (Oct–Mar 10–5). Closed Tue, 1 Jan, 1 May, 25 Dec

♿ Good

✋ Moderate

Silver-cream horses – one of the classic sights of the Camargue

3
Fondation Maeght, St-Paul-de-Vence

✝ 83A3

✉ St-Paul-de-Vence

☎ 04 93 32 81 63

🕐 Oct–Jun, 10–12:30, 2:30–6; Jul–Sep, 10–7

🍽 Café

♿ Few

✋ Very expensive

↔ St-Paul-de-Vence (➤ 89), Vence (➤ 90), Cagnes-sur-Mer (➤ 84)

❓ Cinema, gift shop and art library

'A world in which modern art can both find its place and that otherworldliness which used to be called supernatural.'

These words were spoken by André Malraux, minister of cultural affairs, during the opening of Foundation Maeght in 1964, a beautiful gallery which has since become one of the most distinguished modern-art museums in the world. It was the brainchild of Aimé and Marguerite Maeght, who were art dealers and close friends of Matisse, Miró, Braque, Bonnard and Chagall, and it was their private collection that formed the basis of the museum. Their aim was to create an ideal environment in which to display contemporary art, and to achieve this they worked in close collaboration with the Catalan architect, José-Luis Sert.

The small artful gallery which resulted is hidden amid umbrella pines above the quaint hilltop village of St-Paul-de-Vence. It is surrounded by a small park which contains a collection of sculptures, mosaics and murals. The building itself blends into its natural surroundings, with massive windows, light traps in the roof, and extraordinary white cylindrical 'sails' atop the building. These are not solely decorative, but serve the dual purpose of collecting rainwater to work the fountains.

The Fondation Maeght's remarkable permanent collection is comprised entirely of 20th-century art and includes works by nearly

The Fondation's garden is a veritable forest of sculptures
Opposite: photogenic Gordes

every major artist of the past 50 years. These are shown in rotation throughout the year except during summer when temporary exhibitions are held. The star sights include the Cour Giacometti – a tiled courtyard peopled with skinny Giacometti figures – Chagall's vast, joyful canvas *La Vie*, Miró's *Labyrinthe*, and a fantastic multi-level maze of fountains, trees, mosaics and sculptures. There is also a chapel in the grounds, which contains stained glass by Braque, Ubec and Marq. It was built in memory of the Maeght's son who died in 1953 at the age of 11. The bookshop and cinema are also worth visiting.

4
Gordes &
the Abbeye de Sénanque

Famous for its artists' colony, magnificent Cistercian abbey and ancient borie *village, Gordes makes an ideal centre for touring the Lubéron.*

Gordes is justifiably rated one of the most beautiful villages in France. Its grandiose church and Renaissance **château** rise from a golden plinth on a spur of Mont Ventoux, surrounded by narrow cobbled streets and tiers of golden sandstone houses that spill down the steep, stony slopes. During World War II many buildings were ruined or abandoned and the village fell into decline until the 1960s, when cubist André l'Hote, constructivist Victor Vasarély and other artists brought new life to the village, restoring the delightful Renaissance houses and setting up attractive galleries, studios and boutiques. The castle currently contains the Museum of Pol Mara, a Flemish contemporary artist and honorary citizen of Gordes.

Just southwest of Gordes, the most famous collection of *bories* in France lie hidden in dusty scrubland. These extraordinary beehive-shaped, dry-stone huts sheltered the earliest farmers and semi-nomadic shepherds as early as the 3rd century BC. This particular **village** at Moulin des Bouillons was inhabited as recently as the last century, and is the largest and most complete of its kind in the world.

In a secluded valley north of Gordes, bathed in a sea of lavender, is one of the great symbols of Provence, the Cistercian abbey of Sénanque – one of France's best remaining examples of 12th-century religious architecture. The monks still follow a secret medieval recipe to concoct a pungent, herb-flavoured yellow liqueur called Sénancole.

🚏 40B1–2

ℹ️ Gordes Tourist Office: Le Château (☎ 04 90 72 02 75)

↔️ Fontaine-de-Vaucluse (► 41), Roussillon (► 24); villages of the Lubéron (► 40, 41, 43)

Château de Gordes

☎ 04 90 72 02 89

🕐 Jul–Aug, daily 10–12, 2–6; Sep–Jun, Wed–Mon 10–12, 2–5. Closed 1 May, 25 Dec

💰 Moderate

Village des Bories

✉️ D2 from Gordes

☎ 04 90 72 03 48

🕐 Daily 9–sunset

♿ Few

💰 Moderate

5
Grand Cañon du Verdon

✚ 69B3

ℹ Verdon Accueil,
Aiguines

☎ 04 94 70 21 64

↔ Aups (► 68); Gréoux-
les-Bains (► 73);
Moustiers-Ste-Marie
(► 74).

❓ Useful contacts: Bureau
des Guides (☎ 04 92
77 30 50) for walkers
and climbers; Ranch
Les Pioneers (☎ 04 92
77 38 30) for horse
riding; Aqua Viva Est
(☎ 04 92 83 75 74) for
canoeing, rafting and
mountain biking; Verdon
Passion (☎ 04 92 74
69 77) for hang-gliding
and biplanes.

*The Cañon boasts some
of the most spectacular
scenery in Provence*

*The deepest, longest, wildest canyon in Europe is
like a dream come true for canoeists, climbers,
white–water rafters and other sports lovers.*

Over the centuries the Verdon river, a tributary of the
mighty Durance, has scored a magnificent gorge in the
limestone plateau of the Alpes-de-Haute-Provence,
stretching a staggering 21km from the Pont de Soleils
down to the vast man-made lake of Ste-Croix. In places it
is over 800m deep, the second deepest gorge in the world
after the Grand Canyon and one of the great natural
wonders of Provence. It was first explored as late as 1905
by Isadore Blanc. Before that people were deterred by
local stories of devils and 'wild men'.

The canyon is best approached from Castellane to the
east. The bed of the canyon is impassable, and the river is
only negotiable by trained sportsmen or with an official
guide. Spectacular winding roads hairpin along the clifftops
on both sides of the gorge, with frequent *belvédères* to
park the car and peer giddily down to the green waters of
the Verdon.

Drivers face a difficult decision whether to follow the
northern Route des Crêtes, with its many magnificent
viewpoints, or the southern Corniche Sublime, through the
ancient hilltop villages of Trigance and Aiguines. Hardened
walkers usually opt for the latter, leaving the road at the
Pont Sublime for an awesome eight-hour trek down into
the gorge through dingy tunnels and along a series of
narrow ledges above the river – not for those with vertigo!
Both car trails take approximately half a day, ending at
Moustiers-Ste-Marie (► 74).

6
Montagne Ste-Victoire

Paul Cézanne was so fascinated by Mont Ste-Victoire that he painted it over 65 times, making this great Provençal landmark famous worldwide.

The Montagne Ste-Victoire lies just east of Aix-en-Provence. Viewed end on, this 16km long silvery ridge (running east–west) takes the form of a shapely pyramid. On its lower red-soil slopes, Coteaux-d'Aix vineyards give way to dense forest, scrub and fragrant herbs. Above the tree line, the limestone peak reflects every hue of light and shadow – blue, grey, white, pink, orange – creating extraordinary designs on the landscape.

✚ 69A2

ℹ️ Aix-en-Provence Tourist Office: 2 place du Général-de-Gaulle (☎ 04 42 16 11 61)

↔️ Aix-en-Provence (➤ 52)

❓ The path to the summit may be closed Jul–Sep due to fire risk.

For Paul Cézanne, native of Aix, the mountain was his favourite local subject. He painted it again and again from all angles and at all hours, creating some of his greatest canvases including *La Montagne Sainte-Victoire* (1904) and *Le Paysage d'Aix* (1905). In a letter to his son in 1906, he wrote 'I spend every day in this landscape, with its beautiful shapes. Indeed, I cannot imagine a more pleasant way or place to pass my time'.

Climbing Mont Ste-Victoire requires stout shoes and sure-footedness as, although not the highest mountain in Provence, it is said to be the steepest. It is a steady two-hour hike from les Cabassols on the D10 to the ruined 17th-century priory and massive Croix de Provence at the 945m summit. At the eastern base of the mountain is Pourrières wood, where the mountain was named following a Roman victory over invading Germanic tribes.

Cézanne's beloved mountain can be seen from afar

21

7

Musée Matisse, Nice

✝ 83B2

✉ 164 avenue des Arènes-de-Cimiez

A truly remarkable collection of Matisse's works, intimate yet instructive and spanning his entire life, housed in a vivid red villa.

Matisse's masterpiece The Rocaille Armchair, *1946*

☎ 04 93 81 08 08

🕐 Apr–Sep, 10–6; Oct–Mar, 10–5. Closed Tue and public hols

🚌 15, 17, 20, 22, 25

♿ Very good

✋ Moderate

↔ Musée Archéologique (➤ 80), Cimiez Monastery (➤ 80)

❓ Guided tours Wed 3:30PM except during school holidays. Three temporary exhibitions a year. Shop

The villa des Arènes is situated on a hill above Nice, at the heart of a 3.6 hectare olive grove in the district of Cimiez (➤ 80) – an exquisite mid-17th century folly, with a cleverly-painted *tromp l'oeil* façade, colonnaded staircases and terraces that are laid out in the Genoese style.

Henri Matisse first came to live in Nice in 1917 and spent long periods of his life near here. Shortly before his death in 1954 he bequeathed his entire personal collection to the city of Nice. Together with a second, even larger donation from his wife in 1960 (including over a hundred personal effects from his studio-apartment in the nearby Hôtel Regina) it formed the basis of a priceless collection, celebrating the life, work and influence of this great artist, and boasting not only the world's largest collection of his drawings, but also all the bronze sculptures that Matisse ever made.

Matisse's entire working life is displayed in the villa, from the initial old-master copies he made during his apprenticeship period, through an era of sober, dark-toned paintings in the 1890s (including *Intérieur à l'harmonium*), to his Impressionist and fauvist phases (*Jeune femme à l'ombrelle* and *Portrait of Madame Matisse*), and beyond to the bright colours and simple shapes of his maturity, best protrayed in his decorative paper cut-outs, silk-screen hangings, and works such as *Nu Bleu IV* and *Nature Morte aux Grenades*.

The large collection of his drawings and engravings (around 450 altogether) are also of particular interest. The book illustrations for James Joyce's *Ulysses* and the powerful sketches and stained-glass models for the Chapelle du Rosaire at Vence (➤ 90) should definitely not be missed.

8
Musée Picasso, Antibes

Picasso once had a studio inside this seafront château. Today it houses one of the world's finest collections of his works.

The Grimaldi dynasty ruled for centuries in this beautiful 12th- to 16th-century château, constructed following the design of a Roman fort and occupying a strategic site overlooking the ramparts. In 1928, the city of Antibes acquired the castle to house a museum of art, history and archaeology. When in 1946 Pablo Picasso returned to his beloved Mediterranean, having spent the war years in Paris, he found that he had nowhere suitable to work. The mayor of Antibes lent him a room in Château Grimaldi for use as an atelier and in gratitude Picasso left his entire output of that period on permanent loan to the castle museum, together with a collection of lively ceramics, tapestries and sculptures that he later created in the nearby village of Vallauris. More of his work can be seen in the two museums there.

Although Picasso only spent six months in Antibes it was one of his most prolific periods. After the melancholy of war, his work here took on a new dimension, reflecting the *joie de vivre* of the Mediterranean, bathed in sunny colours and incandescent light. He combined bold new techniques – using industrial paints, fibro-cement and plywood – with ancient themes and mythical images, creating such masterpieces as *Le centaur et le Navire, Ulysee et les Sirènes, Nu couché au lit bleu* and his famous *La Joie de Vivre*.

Most of Picasso's works can be found on the first floor of the castle. Works by his contemporaries, including Léger, Modigliani and Max Ernst, hang on the second floor (Picasso's former studio), and the ground floor contains photographs of the great master at work. On a sunny terrace overlooking the sea, stone and bronze sculptures by Miró, Richier and Pagès are strikingly displayed among cacti, trees and flowers.

✚ 83A2

✉ Château Grimaldi, place Mariéjol

☎ 04 92 90 54 20

🕐 15 Jun–15 Sep 10–6; 16 Sep–14 Jun 10–12, 2–6. Closed Mon and public hols

🖐 Moderate

↔ Biot (► 84), Cagnes (► 84), Cannes (► 85), Mougins (► 89)

❓ Guided tours on request. Children's workshops (phone for details)

Picasso's bold and innovative use of line and colour can be seen at the Musée Picasso

9
Roussillon

✚ 40B1

ℹ️ Roussillon Tourist
Office: place de la Poste
(☎ 04 90 05 60 25)

🍴 David (▶ 93)

♿ Good (lower village);
few (upper village)

↔ Gordes (▶ 19); villages
of the Lubéron (▶ 38)

❓ Ochre festival held in
May (during Ascension
weekend)

*It is easy to fall in love with Roussillon, once
known worldwide for its ochre dyes, now
considered one of France's most beautiful villages.*

This unforgettable village is perched on a platform of rich
rust rock called Mont Rouge, surrounded by jagged cliffs
and hollows of every shade of ochre imaginable from
blood red, gold, orange and pale yellow to white, pink and
violet, hidden amid dark pine forests and scrub. For here lie
the richest deposits of ochre in all France.

The village of Roussillon was founded by Raymond
d'Avignon. According to legend, one day he discovered his
wife was having an affair with his page-boy. He killed the
page and served his heart on a platter to his wife. Greatly
distressed, she leapt off the cliffs: her blood formed a
spring, permanently colouring the surrounding soil and
creating some of the most spectacular scenery in the
whole of Provence, from the spiky multi-coloured needles
of the 'Valley of Fairies' to the brilliantly hued 'Cliffs of

Blood' and deep gullies of the 'Giant's Causeway'. Here visitors can explore the old opencast quarries along the 1km Sentier des Ocres (Ochre Trail) which has information signboards along the way.

The ochre industry began here at the end of the 18th century, bringing prosperity to the villagers until 1958, when competition from cheap synthetic pigments forced production to stop. Although today very few quarries are worked, Roussillon still holds its merry Ochre Festival at Ascensiontide.

The picturesque houses present a full palette of ochre shades – apricot, pink, violet, gold, mustard, orange, burgundy, russet and brown – creating a special glow in the streets. The hub of the village is the small, lively square beside the Mairie, where the *Roussillonais* gather in the outdoor cafés. Narrow lanes and winding stairways lead up to a Romanesque church, offering a sweeping panorama of the ochreous Vaucluse scenery, with its hill villages and distant mountains.

The Sentier des Ocres is a must for visitors to Roussillon

10
Théâtre Antique, Orange

 39A2

 Place des Frères-Mounet

☎ 04 90 51 17 60

🕐 Jan, Feb, Nov, Dec 9–5; Mar, Oct 9–6; Apr, May, Sep 9–7; Jun–Aug 9–8

 Restricted

✋ Expensive, but also valid for Musée Municipal

↔ Musée de la Ville (► 44)

❓ Telephone for details of guided tours (Jul–Aug only), concert and theatre information

One of the best surviving theatres from the ancient world, built over 2,000 years ago, with seating for up to 10,000 spectators.

The Théâtre Antique was built in the reign of Augustus about AD 1, set into the hillside of Colline St-Eutrope at Arausio. Originally there had been a Celtic settlement here, but under Caesar veterans of the second Gallica legion created a major Roman city, building the magnificent theatre, the triumphal arch, temples, baths and many other public buildings.

Although all that remains of the theatre is a mere shadow of its former splendour, it is nevertheless easy to imagine the theatre in its heyday. The *cavea*, or tiered semicircle, was divided into three levels according to rank. On one tier you can still see the inscription *EQ GIII* meaning 'Equus Gradus III' or 'third row for horsemen!' Senators and guests of honour would occupy marble seats in front of the first row.

The monumental stage wall (*frons scanae*), made from red sandstone and measuring 103m long, 37m high and nearly 2m thick, is the only one in the world to survive completely from ancient times. Louis XIV described it as 'the greatest wall in my kingdom'. Once decorated with 76 columns, friezes, niches and statues, today all the statues have vanished except an imposing marble figure of Emperor Augustus. Beneath the statue is the central 'Royal door', and within the wall were hidden passageways enabling actors and stagehands to move about unseen. For the same purpose the wooden stage had numerous trap doors. Originally the theatre was used for meetings, lectures, theatre and concerts. Its excellent acoustics are demonstrated every July and August in the Chorégies, a world-famous festival of opera, drama and ballet, held here since 1869. Classical, jazz and pop concerts are also held here throughout the summer.

Perched high above the stage, it is easy to step back to Roman times

To the west of the theatre, Colline St-Eutrope is well worth the climb to reach its cool, shady park with magnificent views over Orange, the theatre and the Rhône plain beyond.

What
to See

Above: *Aups is an attractive agricultural town*
Right: *road marker in the mountains*

27

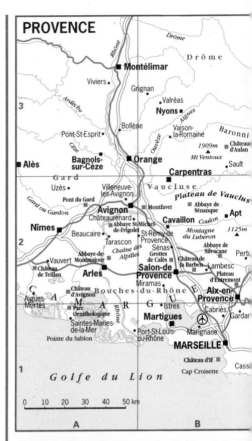

PROVENCE

*Mauve corduroy fields of
lavender stripe the
landscape*

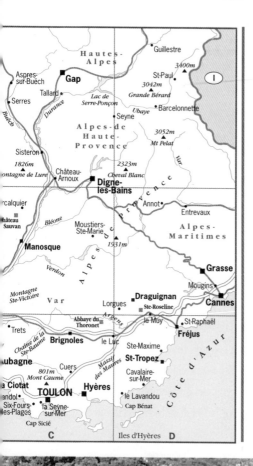

Hautes-Alpes

Guillestre

Aspres-sur-Buëch

Gap

St-Paul

3400m ▲

Serres

Tallard

Durance

Lac de Serre-Ponçon

3042m
Grande Bérard

Barcelonnette

Ubaye

Seyne

A l p e s - d e - H a u t e - P r o v e n c e

3052m
Mt Pelat

Sisteron

1826m
Montagne de Lure

Château-Arnoux

2323m
Cheval Blanc

Digne-les-Bains

Var

alquier

Château Sauvan

Bléone

Annot

Entrevaux

Moustiers-Ste-Marie

Alpes-Maritimes

Manosque

1931m ▲

Verdon

Grasse

Montagne Ste-Victoire

V a r

Lorgues

Draguignan

Ste-Roseline

Mougins

Cannes

Trets

Argens

Abbaye du Thoronet

le Muy

St-Raphaël

Chaîne de la Ste-Baume

Brignoles

le Luc

Fréjus

ubagne

Cuers

Ste-Maxime

St-Tropez

C ô t e   d ' A z u r

801m
Mont Caume ▲

Massif des Maures

Cavalaire-sur-Mer

a Ciotat

TOULON

Hyères

andol

Six-Fours-les-Plages

la Seyne-sur-Mer

le Lavandou

Cap Bénat

Cap Sicié

C

Iles d'Hyères

D

Vaucluse

Despite being one of France's smallest *départe-ments*, the Vaucluse has been blessed with more than its fair share of beautiful scenery and treasures. A region of colourful, bustling markets, swift-flowing rivers, sweetly scented *garrigue*, brilliant red and yellow ochre cliffs, and world-famous wines. The timeless quality of its sun-bleached landscapes is reinforced by some of the finest Roman remains, at Orange and Vaison-la-Romaine, and the entire region is saturated in medieval buildings, from the remotest *village perché* to the papal grandeur of Avignon.

For many the Lubéron region epitomises the real magic of Provence – timeless villages dozing under blue skies, ornamental fountains splashing in the sleepy squares and villagers playing boules under shady plane trees or enjoying a simple meal while gazing out over silvery olive groves, scented fig trees and neat rows of lavender.

'It is a land of milk and honey, the best milk and the most perfumed honey, where all the good things of the earth overflow and are cooked to perfection.'

WILLIAM BOLITHO
(*Camera Obscura*)

Avignon

The city of Avignon – administrative centre of the Vaucluse and a major artistic centre – is one of the most important cities in the history of France. Strategically located near the junction of the Rhône and Durance rivers, it has been the scene of countless conflicts since Roman times, and for over a century it was the seat of the popes and centre of a religious and political power struggle.

It was a French pope, Clement V, who first moved his residence from the Vatican to Avignon in 1309. From then on a succession of French popes and cardinals built up a powerful base here, constructing a cornucopia of architectural treasures within the city's massive fortifications to display their wealth and power. Following pressure from the rest of Europe, the papal establishment finally transferred back to Rome in 1377. However, a group of French cardinals refused to accept this and elected a series of rival antipopes who, over the next 40 years, continued to exercise authority from Avignon, creating what is today known as the Great Schism.

A walk along the ramparts reveals the two sides of Avignon today – the village-like atmosphere of the historic walled old town, its skyline adorned with steeples and monuments, and the sprawling factories and bustling modern suburbs beyond, accommodating the city's 100,000 inhabitants. It is a cheerful, lively tourist centre, especially in July when the narrow lanes and pedestrian zones resound with buskers, street theatre and café cabarets during the renowned arts festival (➤ 60).

➕ 28A2

ℹ Avignon Tourist Office:
41 cours Jean-Jaurés
(☎ 04 32 74 32 74)

↔ Carpentras (➤ 40);
Cavaillon (➤ 41);
Châteauneuf-du-Pape
(➤ 35); Orange (➤ 44);
Tarascon (➤ 58)

The Palais des Papes, an imposing sight above the Rhône river

➕ 32B2
✉ 5 rue du Laboureur
☎ 04 90 82 29 03
🕐 Wed–Sun 1–6. Also open
Tue from mid-Apr to mid-
Oct.
✋ Moderate

➕ 32B2
✉ 65 rue Joseph Vernet

*Avignon's main square,
Place de l'Horloge,
is always a lively meeting-
place*

What to See in Avignon

FONDATION ANGLADON-DUBRUJEAUD ●●

This new museum in an elegant city mansion boasts the
prestigious collection of artists Jean and Paulette
Angladon-Dubrujeaud, including paintings by Sisley,
Manet, Cézanne and Picasso and Provence's only original
van Gogh.

MUSÉE CALVET ●

The private art collection of physician Dr Esprit Calvet
(1728–1810) provides a comprehensive study of the

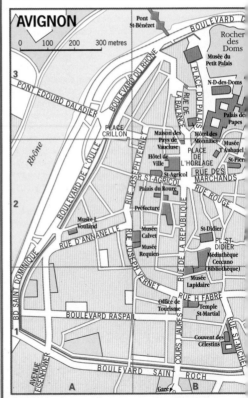

French and Avignon schools of painting and sculpture from the 15th to 20th centuries, including works by David, Delacroix, Modigliani and Manet.

PALAIS DU ROURE ✪

Until the end of the last century, this Florentine-style palace was the office of Frédérick Mistral's Provençal-language magazine *L'Aïoli*. Today it is a beautiful museum of Provençal history, arts, literature and traditions.

PLACE DE L'HORLOGE ✪✪

A lively square, abuzz with cafés, artists and buskers.

☎ 04 90 86 33 84
🕐 10–1, 2–6 (7 in summer) Wed–Mon
♿ Good 💷 Expensive

✚ 32B2
✉ 3 rue du Collège-du-Roure
☎ 04 90 80 80 88
🕐 Tue at 3PM; daily in Jul
♿ Few 💷 Moderate

✚ 32B2

The shady gardens of the Rochers des Doms offer a cool retreat for a picnic

32B3
✉ Place du Palais
☎ 04 90 27 50 00
🕐 Nov to mid-Mar
9:30–5:45; mid-Mar to
Oct 9–7 (9 in Jul, 8 in Aug
and Sep)
🍴 Café in summer months
♿ Few
💶 Expensive
↔ Petit Palais (➤ below)
❓ Guided tours ☎ 04 90
27 50 73

PALAIS DES PAPES ✪✪✪

The majestic, monumental Pope's Palace was built in a spacious cobbled square as a symbol of the papal residency in Avignon. Its massive walls shelter a labyrinth of halls, courtyards and chambers divided into the Old Palace, built by Pope Benedict XII between 1334 and 1342, and the New Palace, begun under his successor, Pope Clement VI and completed in 1348. Each part has its own distinctive character. Benedict XII's Old Palace has an almost austere, monastic simplicity in stark contrast with the New Palace.

Clement VI enjoyed the high life and was an ardent patron of the arts, displaying his wealth and power in lavish frescoes and flamboyant ceilings. His ostentatious New Palace received a mixed reception. Medieval chronicler Froissart pronounced it 'the finest and strongest palace in the world' whereas Petrach called it 'Unholy Babylon … a sewer where all the filth of the universe has gathered'. The entire complex is so vast that it has been described as 'a city within a city' and takes at least a day to visit. Don't miss the fanciful Audience Hall, the frescoes of the Stag Room, the princely papal bedroom, St Martial's Chapel and the Hall of the Consistory.

✚ 32B3
✉ Place du Palais
☎ 04 90 86 44 58
🕐 Oct–May 9:30–1, 2–5:30;
Jun–Sep 10–1, 2–6.
Closed Tue
♿ Few 💶 Expensive
↔ Palais des Papes
(➤ above)

PETIT PALAIS ✪✪

The beautifully restored former residence of the bishops of Avignon was converted in 1958 to house two important collections – medieval works from the Musée Calvet and the Campana collection of 13th- to 16th-century Italian paintings from the Louvre. The medieval works include 600 sculptures and around 60 paintings, such as the *Retable Requin* by Enguerrand Quarton.

✚ 32B3
✉ Rue Ferruce
☎ 04 90 27 51 16
🕐 Nov to mid-Mar
9:30–5:45; mid-Mar to
Oct 9–7 (closes 9 in Jul, 8
in Aug & Sep)
♿ None 💶 Moderate
↔ Petit Palais (➤ above);
Rocher des Doms (➤ 33)

PONT ST-BÉNÉZET ✪✪

This famous bridge, immortalised in the popular children's song *Sur le pont d'Avignon,* was one of the first bridges built across the Rhône. Originally made of wood, it was

reconstructed in stone at the end of the 13th century. Only four of its original 22 arches remain, together with the tiny chapel of St Nicholas on the second pier. The song by an anonymous composer is famous worldwide. However, it was under the arches of the bridge (*sous le pont*), on the Île de la Barthelasse, that the people of Avignon used to dance.

'Sur le pont d'Avignon, on y danse, on y danse…'

*The rolling vineyards of
Beaumes-de-Venise*

Côtes du Rhône Villages

The stony, sun-baked red-clay soil of the southern Rhône nurtures some of France's most prestigious wines – fine and full-bodied with a spicy bouquet, of which the best known is Châteauneuf-du-Pape. Numerous wine routes lead you through charming yellow-stone villages with shady squares, old fountains and red-tiled roofs, hidden in a sea of vineyards and largely given over to restaurants and cellars offering free wine tasting.

BEAUMES-DE-VENISE ✪✪

Majestically framed by the lacy silver crags of the Dentelles de Montmirail, Beaumes is well-known for its sweet golden Muscat wines. Taste them at the Cave des Vignerons or during the region's annual wine festivals accompanied by goats' cheeses, *foie gras* and melons drowned in Muscat.

🔶 40B2
ℹ️ Tourist Office: Place du Marché (☎ 04 90 62 94 39)
↔️ Carpentras (➤ 40)

CHÂTEAUNEUF-DU-PAPE ✪✪✪

The wines of Châteauneuf-du-Pape are world-renowned, largely thanks to 13th-century Pope Jean XXII of Avignon. It was he who built the now-ruined château, with its splendid views, as a summer residence and planted the first vineyards. Many Côtes du Rhône wines are made from just one grape variety, but vintners here blend up to 13 different grapes to produce their distinctive wines of unique complexity. The Musée du Père Anselme here is dedicated to the history of local viticulture and visitors can indulge in wine tastings.

🔶 40A2
ℹ️ Tourist Office: place du Portail (☎ 04 90 83 71 08)
↔️ Orange (➤ 44)
❓ Wine festival: first weekend in Aug

GIGONDAS ✪✪

The wines of this small, unspoiled village, set against the jagged backdrop of the Dentelles, are reputed to be the best in the area, notably the intense red Grenache wines.

🔶 40B2
ℹ️ Tourist Office: place du Portail (☎ 04 90 65 85 46)

SÉGURET ✪✪✪

This charming circular hilltop village has its own *appellation d'origine contrôlée*. The ochre cottages, with their turquoise shutters hidden behind vines and creeper, house craftsmen renowned for their dried flowers and *santons* (terracotta Christmas crib figurines).

🔶 40B2
✉️ Tourist Office: Vaison-la-Romaine, place du Chanoine-Sautel (☎ 04 90 36 02 11)
↔️ Vaison-la-Romaine (➤ 45)

Food & Drink

France is universally recognised as the world leader in the field of food and wine, and of all its great regional styles *la cuisine Provençale* has one of the strongest personalities; spicy Mediterranean dishes with bold, sun-drenched flavours as varied as its landscapes, leaning heavily on olive oil, tomatoes, garlic and wild herbs. As Peter Mayle remarked: 'Everything is full-blooded. The food is full of strong, earthy flavours … There is nothing bland about Provence.' (*A Year in Provence*)

Provençal specialities include *soupe au pistou* (vegetable soup with garlic, basil and cheese); *beignets de courgettes* (courgette flowers dipped in batter and deep fried), *mesclun* (a hearty salad including dandelion and hedge-mustard leaves), *daube* (beef stew with red wine, cinnamon and lemon peel), *salade Niçoise* (with tuna, egg, black olives and anchovies) and *pain bagnat* (Niçoise salad inside a loaf of bread).

Cuisine Niçoise

Within the Provençal tradition, the Nice area has its own distinctive cuisine, reflecting the town's former association

Aix-en-Provence's markets are famous throughout the region

with Italy. Indeed, pizzas and pastas taste every bit as good in Menton and Nice as they do over the border. Look out also for *pissaladière* (olive and onion pizza), *socca* (thin pancake made of chickpea flour), *petits farcis* (savoury stuffed artichoke hearts, courgettes and tomatoes) and *estocaficada* (stockfish stew).

Surf and Turf

Near the coast fish dishes reign supreme. Expect to pay at least F250 for an authentic bouillabaisse (▶ 95), or else try *bourride*, poor man's fish soup. *Moules frites* (mussels with french fries) are always good value, as are *tellines Camarguais*, tiny shellfish served with *aïoli* (garlic mayonnaise). By contrast, meat dishes predominate inland. Try Sisteron lamb with its taste of wild thyme, game dishes, *boeuf gardian* (a spicy beef stew with olives, served with Camarguais rice) or frogs legs *à la Provençale* (in a tomato and garlic sauce). And don't forget the tasty mountain cheeses, lavender-scented honey and truffles.

Vin de Provence

About 11 per cent of France's wine comes from Provence. The chalky soils and warm dry Mediterranean climate lend themselves to the development of the smooth, easy-to-drink wines such as Côtes du Ventoux and Côtes du Lubéron. Some of the more famous labels include Côtes du Rhône (▶ 35), notably Gigondas, Vacqueyras and Châteauneuf-du-Pape, a full-bodied, robust wine with a powerful, complex bouquet, perfect with red meats and cheeses.

Provence is particularly famous for its rosé wines, fresh, crisp and fruity, and an ideal accompaniment to seafood. Côtes de Provence and Côteaux d'Aix are numbered among the best. For white wine try the dry, green-tinged Cassis wines (▶ 94) or the fruity Bellet, one of Provence's most original wines and, with only 20 producers, much prized by connoisseurs (▶ 109). Other specialist wines of the region include Listel, a cloudy 'grey' rosé and the golden, sultana-flavoured dessert wine, Muscat de Beaumes-de-Venise (▶ 35).

Sweet Things
For those with a sweet tooth there are juicy Cavaillon melons, *pain d'épice* (spiced bread), delicious crystallized fruits and a medley of candies including burnt-sugar Berlingots from Carpentras and Calissons d'Aix. In 1994 the village of Sault entered the Guinness Book of Records with the world's biggest bag of nougat, 3m high and filled with 40,000 pieces!

Some of Provence's best wines come from the Lubéron near Menerbes

⊞ 40C1
Parc Naturel Régional du Lubéron
🛈 Maison du Parc, place Jean-Jaurès, Apt (☎ 04 90 04 42 00)
🕐 Mon–Sat, 8:30–12, 1:30–6 (till 7 Apr–Sep)

⊞ 40C1
🛈 Tourist Office: 20 avenue Philippe-de-Girard (☎ 04 90 74 03 18)
⬌ Roussillon (► 24)

Above: a small fountain in central Apt

⊞ 40B1
🛈 Tourist Office: 7 place Carnot (☎ 04 90 75 91 90)
⬌ Lacoste (► 43)

The Lubéron

The Parc Naturel Régional du Lubéron is a protected region of cedar and pine countryside interspersed with lavender fields, almond and olive groves, fragrant herbs, *garrigue* scrub and vineyards, draped across a compact range of small mountains that stretch from Cavaillon to Manosque.

The dramatic wooded gorge of the Combe de Lourmarin (road D943) splits the region in two. The high, wild Grand Lubéron mountains lie to the east. Walkers tackling the strenuous climb from Auribeau to the uppermost peak of Mourre Nègre (1,100m) will be well rewarded with dizzy views from the Basse-Alpes to the Mediterranean. To the west, the pretty *villages perchés* of the Petit Lubéron have long been one of France's most fashionable *residences secondaires*, even before Peter Mayle's bestseller, *A Year in Provence*!

APT ✪

This busy old market town north of the Lubéron mountains makes an ideal centre for touring the area. The best place to start is at the Maison du Parc Naturel Régional du Lubéron, which details walks and other outdoor activities, together with a small museum documenting local natural history.

The town itself is surrounded by fruit trees. Hardly surprisingly it is renowned for its jams and claims to be the 'world capital of crystallized fruit'! Try some for yourself along with other tempting Provençal specialities at the bustling Saturday market, always a jolly affair with barrel organs and buskers. Apt is also well known for its lavender essence and handmade pottery and is an important centre for the truffle trade in winter.

BONNIEUX ✪✪

The terracotta-roofed houses of Bonnieux wind up to a tiny 12th-century chapel surrounded by sentinel-like cypresses. The village is spread out on a north-facing spur of the Petit Lubéron overlooking the vineyards, cherry trees and lavender fields of the Coulon valley, and its belvedere commands entrancing views over the Plateau de Vaucluse to mighty Mont Ventoux beyond. Once papal property, Bonnieux has preserved many fine monuments including the Town Hall, a bakery museum and some notable Renaissance paintings in its two churches.

GORDES (➤ 19, TOP TEN)

LOURMARIN ✪✪

The imposing Renaissance château, the medieval houses made from local yellow stone and dressed in honeysuckle, tiny fountain-filled squares and a host of inviting restaurants create a picturesque ensemble on the southern slopes of the Lubéron. French novelist and philosopher Albert Camus bought a house here after winning the Nobel Prize for literature in 1957. His simple grave can be visited in the village cemetery.

✚ 40C1
ℹ Tourist Office: 9 avenue Philippe-de-Girard (☎ 04 90 68 10 77)
↔ Bonnieux (➤ 38)

MÉNERBES ✪✪

The Luberón's highest-profile village has long attracted celebrities, including Picasso's mistress Dora Maar and more recently Mitterand and Peter Mayle. Sadly, this scenic, once off-the-beaten-track village, perched high above neat rows of vines in the Petit Lubéron, has suffered from its association with Mayle (who lived in a *mas* near by until he was driven away by hoards of visiting fans!) Nevertheless, it remains a lively working village with a dynamic weekly market, 13th-century fortress and 14th-century church.

✚ 40B1
ℹ Bonnieux Tourist Office (➤ 38)
↔ Oppéde-le-Vieux (➤ 39), Bonnieux (➤ 38), Lacoste (➤ 43)

OPPÈDE-LE-VIEUX ✪✪

At first glimpse Oppède appears a typical Provençal village of narrow streets, stairways and attractive cream-coloured houses tumbling down the hillside, all crowned by an impressive ruined château. On closer inspection you will see that many of the houses are gutted ruins, overrun with weeds. The village was abandoned in the late 19th century, following the tyrannical reign of Baron Oppède who sold over 800 villagers as slaves in Marseille. In recent years some of the quaint old cottages and the Romanesque church have been restored by resident artists and Oppède is returning to its former glory.

✚ 40B1
↔ Cavaillon (➤ 41), Menerbes (➤ 40)

Beautiful Bonnieux tumbles down the hillside in the Petit Lubéron

What else to See in Vaucluse

CARPENTRAS ✪

40B2

Tourist Office: place
Aristide Briand (☎ 04
90 63 00 78)

Côtes du Rhône villages
(➤ 35), Orange (➤ 44),
Vaison-la-Romaine
(➤ 45), Venasque
(➤ 45)

Cathédrale St-Siffrein

✉ place Générale-de-Gaulle
☎ 04 90 63 08 33
🕐 Daily 8–12, 2–6

Synagogue

✉ Place de la Mairie
☎ 04 90 63 39 97
🕐 Mon–Thu 10–12, 3–5, Fri
10–12, 3–4. Closed Sat,
Sun, hols and Jewish
hols
🎟 Free

*Carpentras market – a
taste of Provence*

This prosperous market town, at the heart of the Côtes du Ventoux wine region, was the old capital of Venasque (then called the Comtat Venaissin) from the 14th century until the Revolution. Situated beside the Auzon river amid rich farmland, it is well known throughout the region for its Friday morning market, when the shady plane-tree lined avenues of the old town are filled with the colours and fragrances of Provence alongside Carpentras's own specialities – truffles, candied fruits and the stripy boiled sweets called *berlingots*.

In the heart of town a small triumphal arch with vivid carvings of chained prisoners marks the Roman period at Carpentras, whereas the nearby Porte d'Orange is the only surviving part of the medieval ramparts. Other notable buildings include the Gothic **Cathédrale St-Siffrein** and France's oldest **synagogue**, which dates back to 1327.

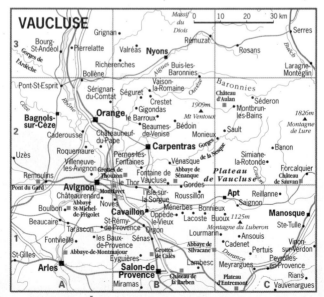

CAVAILLON ✪

Cavaillon is France's greatest market garden – its very name synonymous with those delicious, sweet, pink-fleshed melons – and boasts one of Europe's largest wholesale fruit and vegetable markets. The vast, mouth-watering market for the general public every Monday morning is considered the most important market in the Vaucluse.

The town's agricultural wealth stems from its location in the fertile Durance valley. From the Colline St-Jacques, a one-time neolithic site at the top of the town, there are spectacular views across the valley to the distant highlands of the Lubéron and the Alpilles. Back in the town centre, numerous Roman finds have been assembled in the Musée Archéologique. The former cathedral is also worth visiting, as is the beautifully preserved 18th-century synagogue, with its small museum illustrating the region's traditional protection of Jewish communities.

🚩 40B1
ℹ️ Tourist Office: place François-Tourel (☎ 04 90 71 32 01)
↔️ Oppède-le-Vieux (➤ 39), Fontaine-de-Vaucluse (➤ 41), Eygalières (➤ 56), Gordes (➤ 19)

FONTAINE-DE-VAUCLUSE ✪✪✪

Tucked away at the end of the narrow *vallis clausa* (enclosed valley), after which the whole Vaucluse *département* is named, Fontaine-de-Vaucluse is famous for its emerald-green spring, which gushes from a huge cave-like abyss at the foot of a 230m cliff. Research has proved that this is one of the world's largest and most powerful springs. It consists of a vast underground labyrinth of rivers covering over 2,000sq km and is able to produce up to 200,000 litres of water per second at certain times of year. Pagan Gauls believed it to be the home of a god, while Christians named it the Devil's Hole.

Fontaine's other main tourist attractions include a **paper mill**, the last of a once thriving industry, and a small **museum**, which is dedicated to the famous 14th-century Italian poet Petrarch. He wrote most of his poetry during a 16-year stay here, inspired by the solitude and wilderness he found in the valley.

Below: *tranquil Fontaine-de-Vaucluse, on the Sorgue river*

🚩 40B2
ℹ️ Tourist Office: chemin du Gouffre (☎ 04 90 20 32 22)

Moulin à Paper Vallis Clausa
✉️ Chemin de Gouffre
☎ 04 90 20 34 14
🕐 Daily 9–12:15, 2–6:45. Closed 1 Jan, 25 Dec

Musée Petrach
✉️ Left bank of the Sorgue
☎ 04 90 20 37 20
🕐 Apr–May & 1–15 Oct 10–12, 2–6. Jun–Sep 10–12:30, 1:30–6. Closed Tue and 16 Oct–Mar

40B2

Mont Ventoux
Information: Chalet
d'Accueil du Mont
Ventoux (☎ 04 90 63 42
02)

Carpentras (► 40),
Vaison-la-Romaine
(► 45)

Organised hikes with
Rando-Ventoux Centre
Régional de la Randonnée
(☎ 04 90 65 63 95 –
Bedoin Tourist Office) to
the summit for sunrise

MONT VENTOUX ✪✪

The awesome, isolated massif of Mont Ventoux – the 'Giant of Provence' – rises a lofty 1,901m above the Plateau de Vaucluse, making it the highest peak between the Alps and the Pyrénées. Italian poet Francesco Petrarch was the first recorded man to reach its summit in 1336. It is a good 5-hour hike, but today most people cheat and drive up to the Col des Tempêtes (1,829m). It is important to wrap up warm because Mont Ventoux (Provençal for windy mountain) does justice to its name. Its bleak limestone peak, totally devoid of vegetation, has been blasted white by icy mistral winds of up to 250kph. For much of the year, the summit is snow-clad, and skiing on its slopes is a popular pastime.

You'll find a game of boules in action in most shady squares

Did you know ?

Boules, southern France's most popular game, is called pétanque *in Provence, from Occitan* pé *(foot) and* tanco *(fixed to the ground).*
The game was born one day in 1901 when arthritic boules player, Jules Le Noir, suggested to his friends that they all play pieds tanqués. *This seemed a good idea and also meant they could return to the village square where they had been previously banned for hitting too many passers-by as they ran and tossed their balls!*
Pétanque is a tactical game – whether to position your ball near the little wooden ball (called a cochonnet *or piglet) or to oust out your opponent's ball. With a flick of the wrist, players sometimes manage both simultaneously.*

A Drive around The Lubéron

Starting in Apt, take the D22 northeast towards Rustrel, then right at the crossroads to Bouvene.

The enormous old ochre quarries of Colorado de Rustrel are a colourful tourist attraction – an almost lunar landscape of mounds, pillars, cliffs and hollows in every imaginable shade of ochre from pale yellow to blood red, set against deep pine forest. (From Bouvene it is a 50-minute walk).

Back at the crossroads, continue straight on along the D179 then the D943 to St-Saturnin-lès-Apt. Leave the village on the D2 to Gordes (► 19). After Gordes, continue along the D2 towards Cavaillon, then take the first left (D103) signposted Apt and Beaumettes. Go straight on at the roundabout, following signs up to the centre of Ménerbes (► 39).

Outside Ménerbes, the Domaine de la Citadelle has a unique museum of corkscrews (Musée du Tire-Bouchon) dating back to the 17th century, along with complimentary wine tasting.

Leave Ménerbes on the D103 then the D109 past the Renaissance abbey of St–Hilaire to Lacoste.

Lacoste vies with neighbouring villages Ménerbes, Bonnieux and Oppède for the title of prettiest Lubéron village – a cinematic *village perché*, rich, exclusive and crowned by an 11th-century fortress which in its heyday was one of the region's grandest.

Further along the D109 you reach Bonnieux (► 38). Leave the village on the D3, then first left (D149) to Pont Julien.

This bridge is reputedly the best-preserved Roman bridge in France.

Turn right at the main road (N100) for the return journey to Apt.

Distance
90 km

Time
2½ hours without stops; full day with visits

Start/end point
Apt
✚ 40C1

Lunch
Le Fournil, Bonnieux (€€)
(► 92)
✉ 5 place Carnot
☎ 04 90 75 83 62

A Lubéron vineyard

40A2

Tourist Office: 5 cours
Aristide-Briand (☎ 04 90
34 70 88)

Carpentras (➤ 40),
Châteauneuf-du-Pape
(➤ 35), Côtes du Rhône
villages (➤ 35), Vaison-la-
Romaine (➤ 45)

Arc de Triomphe

✉ Avenue de l'Arc-de-
Triomphe/N7

Municipal Museum

✉ Rue Madeleine-Roch

☎ 04 90 51 17 60

🕐 Jan, Feb, Nov, Dec 9–5;
Mar, Oct 9–6; Apr, May,
Sep 9–7; Jun, Jul, Aug
9–8

♿ Good

💰 Expensive

Théâtre Antique (➤ 26)

Opposite: *Roman remains
at Vaison-la-Romaine*
Below: *the ancient arch
stands majestically in the
middle of Orange*

ORANGE ✪✪

Historic Orange, the 'Gateway to Provence', lies in the
fertile plain of the Rhône river. Once the Celtic capital of
Arausio, later colonised by veterans of the Roman Second
Legion, its present name dates from the 16th century,
when the town became the property of the House of
Orange. Its main claim to fame are two of the finest
Roman monuments in Europe – the great triumphal arch
and the massive theatre. Today Orange is an important
centre for Côtes du Rhône wines and produce such as
olives, honey and truffles.

The massive 22-m **Arc de Triomphe** was the first
Roman monument to be built on Gallic soil around 20 BC. It
was constructed as a symbol of Roman power following
Caesar's conquest of the Gauls and victory over the Greek
fleet; its three archways are smothered with intricate
carvings depicting naked Gauls bound in chains, victorious
Roman legionaries and a variety of nautical symbols
portraying maritime supremacy. Originally constructed
along the Via Agrippa from Lyon to Arles, today it stands
on a roundabout in the middle of the N7.

The **Municipal Museum** gives a detailed insight into
life in Roman Gaul. The most remarkable exhibit is a huge
marble slab, pieced together from over 400 fragments to
create a *plan cadastral* (land survey) of the region, detailing
boundaries, land owners and tax rates. There is also a full
history of the city and some interesting portraits of the
royal House of Orange. The museum is a splendid introduction to the Théâtre Antique (➤ 26).

ROUSSILLON (► 24, TOP TEN)

VAISON-LA-ROMAINE

Undisputedly one of Provence's best-preserved Roman sites, Vaison is an extraordinary blend of modern town, medieval village and former Roman city, Vasio Vocontiorum. The richness of its past only emerged in the 20th century when excavations unearthed extensive **Roman remains** including the vast Maison des Messii, with its colonnaded courtyard and mosaic floors, and a Roman theatre (seating 7,000 people during the July arts festival). Visit the Roman city before crossing the 2,000 year old Pont Romain over the jade-green Ouvèze river.

Clinging to a lofty jagged rock above the river, the sand-coloured houses of Vaison's medieval village, draped with knotted vines, creeper and pomegranate bushes, have been lovingly restored by artists and craftsmen. It is a steep climb to the ruined 13th-century château through a maze of twisting cobbled streets, rewarded by sweeping views across Ouvèze Valley and the Côtes du Rhône vineyards as far as the snow-topped Alps.

🖪 40B2

ℹ place du Chanoine-Sautel
   ☎ 04 90 28 76 04

↔ Carpentras (► 40), Côtes
   du Rhône villages
   (► 35), Orange (► 44)

Roman remains

✉ Fouilles de Puymin

🕐 Oct–Mar 10–12, 2–5;
   Apr–May 9:30–12:30,
   2–6; Jun & Sep 9:30–6;
   Jul & Aug 9:30–6:45

♿ Few

🖐 Expensive

❓ Entrance also includes the
   cathedral and cloister

VENASQUE ✪

The lovely ancient village of Venasque, protected by an imposing medieval wall and gateway, enjoys a lofty perch on a steep rock overlooking the Carpentras plain. This formidable site has been occupied since the 6th century, when the bishops of Carpentras sought refuge here from Saracens. It was an episcopal seat for several centuries and a reminder of those times is the remarkable 6th-century **baptistry** (renovated in the 11th century), built on the site of a Roman temple dedicated to Venus. The village also has a considerable gastronomic reputation, and in May and June there is a daily cherry market.

🖪 40B2

ℹ Place de la Mairie (☎ 04
   90 66 11 66)

↔ Gordes (► 19), Carpentras
   (► 40), Fontaine-de-
   Vaucluse (► 41)

Baptistière

✉ Place de l'Église

☎ 04 90 66 62 01

🕐 9–12, 1–6:30 (5 winter).
   Closed mid to end Dec

🖐 Moderate

45

Bouches-du-Rhône

Deep rooted in the customs of old Provence, this was the home of the troubadours, where courtly love developed. Before that, it was the most important part of the Roman Empire outside Italy. At Arles, Glanum and the Baux the region has preserved its monuments, its costumes and its Provençal language.

The entire area is scattered with timeless villages, and honey-coloured farmsteads drenched in bougainvillea and oleander. The landscape varies dramatically, from the lacy limestone peaks of the Alpilles and Cézanne's Montagne St-Victoire to van Gogh's nodding sunflower fields. Beyond is the Camargue, a unique nature reserve where pink flamingos, young bulls and white horses inhabit the marshes.

'I am fascinated with Paris,
its elegance, its women,
even its artificiality.
But with my heart and skin
I love the south —
bullfighting, pleasure, music,
nature, the sea,
goat cheese and bread,
elementary things.'

CHRISTIAN LACROIX

A colourful balcony in the upper town of Vaison-la-Romaine

28A2
Tourist Office: bouldevard
des Lices (☎ 04 90 18
41 20)

Arles

After centuries of fame, first as the Roman capital of Provence, then as a medieval ecclesiastical centre, Arles seemed content to live on its former glory and fine monuments for many years. Recently, however, it has become a lively, popular city, largely due to a variety of new cultural events, including an internationally renowned photographic fair, a rekindled French passion for bullfighting and the influence of local fashion designer, Christian Lacroix, whose imaginative creations reflect the colourful traditional Arlesian costumes (► 105).

For centuries Arles has attracted artists and writers. The beautiful women of the city inspired Daudet's story *L'Arlésienne*, Bizet's opera of the same name and the *farandole*, a medieval dance. Picasso visited to paint the bullfights, and van Gogh moved here in 1888 and lived with Gauguin in the famous yellow house (destroyed in the war), which he immortalised on canvas (*La Maison Jaune*) along with other pictures of Arles including *Café de Nuit* and *Le Pont de Langlois*.

Not only is Arles a city of the arts and an ancient and cultural crossroads, but it is also surrounded by beautiful, varied countryside, making it the perfect centre for exploring the arid Crau plains, the jagged Alpille mountains, the fertile banks of the swift Rhône, and the untamed land of the Camargue (► 17).

Arles' main square, place du Forum, once frequented by van Gogh

A Walk around Arles

Start in Place de la République.

Once the centre of the Roman metropolis, this square is flanked by the cathedral (► 50), the Church of Sainte Anne and the Town Hall.

Leave the square up rue du Cloitre past the Théâtre Antique (► 51). Go right into rue de la Calade, anticlockwise around the Arène (► 50) past place de la Major, then turn right down rue Raspail.

Sunny place de la Major, with its tiny Romanesque church, affords sweeping views across the Crau plain to the Alpille hills and is scene of the famous Fête des Gardians on 1 May (► 60).

Cross rue 4–Septembre into rue de Grille towards the Rhône. Turn right along the river bank past Musée Réattu (entrance in rue du Grand-Prieure) until you reach place Constantin.

Musée Réattu, housed in a 15th-century priory, contains an intriguing set of 57 coloured sketches by Picasso.

Turn left up rue Dominique-Maisto, past the Themes de Constantin, and straight on into rue de l'Hôtel-de-Ville. Turn right at rue des Arènes until you reach place du Forum.

Place du Forum is the heart of Arles and a favourite meeting place for locals and tourists. Note the Corinthian columns embedded into the wall of the Hôtel Nord-Pinus (► 101).

Leave the square along rue du Palais then turn right into rue Balze past the Cryptoportiques. Bear left at rue Mistral then left into the busy pedestrian shopping street, rue de la République, past Museon Arlaton (► 51) and back to place de la République.

Distance
2km

Time
1 hour/full day with visits

Start/end point
Hôtel de Ville, place de la République
➕ 51B1

Arles has a wealth of decorative features such as this fountain

Lunch
La Paillotte (€) (► 95)
✉ 28 rue du Dr-Fanton (north of place du Forum)
☎ 04 90 96 33 15

49

Van Gogh stayed at the Espace Van-Gogh, a local hospital, soon after he cut his ear off

What to See in Arles

LES ALYSCAMPS ⊕⊕

According to custom, the Roman necropolis of Alyscamps (Latin *elisii campi*, elysian fields) was built outside the city walls along the Via Aurelia. Christians took over the cemetery and several miracles are said to have taken place here, including the appearance of Christ. Burial here was so sought after that the dead were sealed in barrels and floated down the Rhône to Arles with a piece of gold between their teeth for the gravedigger. Formerly the necropolis had 19 chapels and several thousand tombs – all that remains is a tranquil poplar-lined alleyway lined with moss-covered tombs.

➕ 51C1
✉ Avenue des Alyscamps
☎ 04 90 49 36 87
⏰ Daily 9–7. Closed 1 Jan, 1 Nov, 25 Dec
♿ Good
💷 Moderate

ARÈNES ⊕⊕⊕

Built during the 1st century AD, this was the largest amphitheatre in Gaul (136m long and 107m wide), able to seat over 20,000 spectators and scene of blood-thirsty contests between gladiators and wild animals. Originally it had three storeys, each with 60 marble-clad arcades, and an awning to protect the audience from the elements. During the Middle Ages the stones from the third level were used to build two churches and 200 houses inside the arena to shelter the poor. These were demolished in 1825, leaving the amphitheatre once again free for bullfights.

➕ 51C2
✉ Rond-Point des Arènes
☎ 04 90 49 36 86
⏰ May–Oct 9–6, Nov–Feb 10–4:30, Apr 9–5:30. Closed 1 Jan, 1 Nov, 25 Dec and for occasional bullfights
♿ Few
💷 Moderate
↔ Théâtre Antique (➤ 51)

ÉGLISE ST-TROPHIME ⊕⊕

A masterpiece of Provençal Romanesque. The original church was built in the 5th century, then rebuilt at the end of the 11th century, and the ornate tympanum, depicting the Last Judgement, was added in the next century. By contrast, the austerity of the interior is striking. The cloister of St-Trophime, with rich carvings and sensitively illuminated chapels hung with Aubusson tapestries, is among the treasures of Provence.

➕ 51B2
✉ Place de la République
☎ 04 90 96 07 38
⏰ Daily 8:30–6:30. Cloister: Apr–Sep 9–7; Oct–Mar 10–4:30
♿ Few
💷 Cloister: moderate
↔ Théâtre Antique (➤ 51)

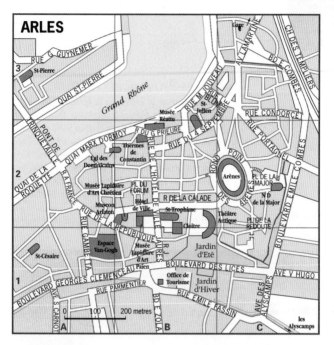

ARLES

ESPACE VAN-GOGH ✪✪

It was in Arles that Vincent van Gogh cut off his ear and gave it to a surprised prostitute! Arles was outraged and was greatly relieved when he voluntarily entered the local hospital in 1889. Its garden has been restored to match the Dutch artist's descriptions.

✚ 51A1
✉ Rue Président-Wilson
☎ 04 90 49 39 39
◷ Courtyard always open
♿ Good
▯ Free

MUSÉE DE L'ARLES ANTIQUE ✪✪✪

This splendid museum is an absolute must see. It is built over the Cirque Romaine, an enormous 2nd century chariot racecourse, which has recently been excavated. It is a modern museum covering the history of the area from Roman rule to the Christian era.

✚ West of city centre
✉ Presqu'île du Cirque-Romain
☎ 04 90 18 88 88
◷ Mar–Oct 9–7, Nov–Feb 10–5. Closed some hols
♿ Excellent ▯ Moderate

MUSÉON ARLATEN ✪

Poet Frédéric Mistral founded the Muséon Arlaten in 1896, thus promoting a Provençal renaissance in Arles. It illustrates everyday life in the region and includes a beautiful exhibition of Arlésien costume, still worn on occasions.

✚ 51B2
✉ 29 rue de la République
☎ 04 90 93 58 11
◷ Tue–Sun 9:30–12:30, 2–6, (5 in winter)
♿ None ▯ Moderate

THÉÂTRE ANTIQUE ✪

Sadly, fanatical Christians destroyed a large part of the Roman Antique Theatre (1 BC). Fragments lie forgotten among the bushes and the flowers, suggesting it was once even more lavish than the theatre in Orange (▶ 26).

✚ 51B2
✉ Rue de la Calade
☎ 04 90 49 36 25
◷ 9–6; Oct–Mar 9–12, 2–6
♿ None ▯ Moderate

51

➕ 28B2
ℹ️ Tourist Office: 2 place du Général-de-Gaulle (☎ 04 42 16 11 61)
↔️ Lubéron villages (➤ 38), Aubagne (➤ 56), Marseille (➤ 54)

One of Aix's many fountains

Aix-en-Provence

This old capital of Provence is splashed by nearly 100 fountains, a pleasing reminder that its very name comes from its waters, Aquae Sextiae, as the Romans named it in 123 BC. The city thrived culturally during the Middle Ages under Good King René, an ardent patron of the arts, reaching the height of its splendour during the 17th and 18th centuries, with the construction of over 160 honey-hued *hôtels particuliers* (mansion residences) beautifully decorated with ornamental wrought-iron balconies.

What to see in Aix-en-Provence

➕ 53B4
✉️ 9 avenue Paul-Cézanne
☎ 04 42 21 06 53
🕐 Oct–Mar 10–12, 2–5; Apr to mid-Jun 10–12, 2:30–6; mid-Jun to Sep 10–6
♿ Few 🖐 Moderate
↔️ Cathédrale St-Sauveur (➤ 52)

➕ 53B3

ATELIER PAUL-CÉZANNE ✪✪

Paul Cézanne, Aix's most famous citizen, spent much of his life here, painting the rugged limestone hills of the surrounding countryside (➤ 21). A special circuit *Cézanne* around town, marked by bronze pavement plaques, leads to the studio where he spent the last seven years of his life – poignantly just as he left it, with unfinished canvases, palettes and his old black hat.

CATHÉDRALE ST-SAUVEUR ✪✪

Aix's main church combines a variety of architectural styles: the baptistry is 5th-century, the cloisters

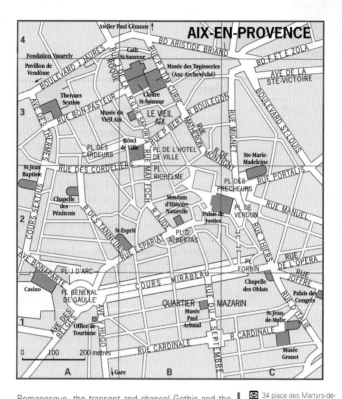

AIX-EN-PROVENCE

Romanesque, the transept and chancel Gothic and the main portal has magnificently carved walnut Renaissance doors. Don't miss Nicolas Froment's famous triptych *Le Buisson Ardent* (1475–6), depicting a vision of the Virgin and Child surrounded by the eternal burning bush of Moses.

COURS MIRABEAU ✪✪✪

This mansion-lined avenue, named after the great revolutionary Comte de Mirabeau and framed by a canopy of plane trees, plays centre stage to the wealthy Aixois society who promenade their poodles here between cups of coffee in *Les Deux Garçons*, and other Parisian-style cafés. The *cours* divides the town centre: The *Vieille Ville* (Old Town) to the north, and the Quartier Mazarin, with its fancy mansions, to the south.

MUSÉE GRANET ✪✪

The city's main museum, housed in the Gothic priory of the Knights of Malta, contains 19th-century Aixois artist François Granet's collection of French, Italian and Flemish paintings. A number of rooms are devoted to local artists, including eight canvases by Cézanne.

⊠ 34 place des Martyrs-de-
la-Résistance
☎ 04 42 23 05 33
♿ Good
⟷ Atelier Paul-Cézanne
(► 52),

✝ 53B1
⊠ Cours Mirabeau
🍴 Pavement cafés
♿ Good
⟷ Musée Granet (► 53)

✝ 53C1
⊠ Place St-Jean-de-Malte
☎ 04 42 38 14 70
🕐 Closed for renovation
until 2005

✚ 28B1
ℹ️ Tourist Office: 4 La
Canebière (☎ 04 91 13
89 00)
🚇 Metro 1: Vieux Port
↔️ Aix-en–Provence (➤ 52),
Aubagne (➤ 56), Cassis
(➤ 57)

Marseille

The extraordinary mix of race and culture in France's premier port and oldest city led Alexandre Dumas to describe Marseille as the 'meeting place of the entire world'. The city has a strong personality, its reputation sustained by political corruption, sporadic gangsterism, and racial tension exacerbated by the National Front. It is also a traditional city, famous for its shipping, its soap, its pastis, the world's largest annual boules competition and the *Marseillaise* (➤ 55); and a city of contradictions and contrasts, from the seedy, congested downtown districts and the hideous high-rise suburbs to the vibrant old port, the sandy beaches and chic residences of the Corniche.

For an overview of the city, visit the Musée du Vieux Marseille and find time to see some of the many architectural gems: the recently discovered Roman Jardin des Vestiges, 5th-century Basilique St-Victor, ostentatious Cathédrale de la Major (1893), the largest to be built in France for many centuries, and Le Corbusier's avant-garde Cité Radieuse (1952, boulevard Michelet) (➤ 101).

Marseille is not an obvious tourist destination and it is admittedly not always easy to find the treasures which lie hidden in this frenetic and sprawling city, but visitors who take the trouble will be richly rewarded.

What to See in Marseille

BASILIQUE DE NOTRE-DAME-DE-LA-GARDE ✪✪

Marseille's major landmark, standing proudly 162m above the city, is a massive neo-Byzantine extravaganza topped by a gaudy golden Madonna. The views over the city are unforgettable, as are the model fishing boats and unusual votive offerings painted by fishermen and sailors inside the church.

✉️ Rue du Fort-du-
Sanctuaire
☎ 04 91 13 40 80
🕐 Oct–May 7–7; Jun–Sep
7–8
🚌 60 ♿ Good
🎫 Free

LA CANEBIÈRE ✪

🚌 7, 8, 31, 33, 34, 80, 81

The main thoroughfare of Marseille took its name from the Provençal *canébe* (cannabis), originally running from former hemp fields to the rope-making heart of the old port. Once considered the Champs Élysées of Marseille, lined with fancy shops, grand cafés and luxury hotels, it has since lost much of its former grandeur, but remains very much *the* place for shopping.

CHATEAU D'IF ✪✪

This forbidding fortress castle lies 3km offshore on the barren, rocky Île du Frioul. Its long history represents an extraordinary blend of fact, fiction and legend. Built in 1528 by François I to protect the port, it later became a prison, with famous inmates including the legendary Man in the Iron Mask and also Alexander Dumas' fictional Count of Monte Cristo.

✚ 28B1
☎ 04 91 59 02 30
🕐 Daily 9:30–5:30 or 6. Closed Mon Oct–Mar
🍴 Café (€)
🚢 Quai des Belges (☎ 04 91 55 50 09)
♿ Few 💷 Moderate

PALAIS LONGCHAMP – MUSÉE DES BEAUX-ARTS ✪✪

This grandiose 1860s palace houses Marseille's main art gallery, packed with masterpieces by Rubens, Brueghel, Corot and local Marseille artists.

✉ Palais Longchamp, 4e
☎ 04 91 14 59 30
🕐 10–5. Closed Mon and hols
Ⓜ Metro 1: Longchamp–Cinq-Avenues
♿ Good
💷 Cheap

Did you know?

During the French Revolution 500 volunteers were sent from Marseille to Paris. As they marched northwards, they sang a song, recently composed by Rouget de Lisle in Strasbourg. By the time they reached Paris, it had been adopted as the anthem of the revolution, and was named La Marseillaise *in honour of the city's 'choir'.*

Colourful fishing boats clutter the Vieux Port

28A2

Les Baux-de-Provence
Tourist Office: Passage
Porte Mage (☎ 04 90 54
34 39)

Arles (►48), St-Rémy-
de-Provence (►58)

Les-Baux-de-Provence
Citadelle

Ville Morte

04 90 54 55 56

Daily: spring 9–7:30;
summer 9–9; autumn
9–6:30; winter 9–5

Expensive

Musée du Vieil

Chapelle des Pénitents

04 90 95 91 52

Mid-Mar to Oct, Sun 3–6

Few

Free

29C1

Tourist Office: avenue
Antide-Boyer
(☎ 04 42 03 49 98)

Marseille (►54), Cassis
(►57)

What to See in Bouches-du-Rhône

LES ALPILLES ✪✪✪

South of St-Rémy-de-Provence lies a thirsty landscape of crumpled white limestone crags – the Chaîne des Alpilles. Market gardens, vineyards and long avenues of plane trees on the lower slopes give way to olive groves, and scrub splashed with yellow broom, lilac lavender and scented wild thyme. This area is easy to explore on foot, horseback or bike, and you are unlikely to meet anyone except the occasional flock of sheep!

Often called 'the Pompeii of Provence', the ancient ruined **citadel of les Baux-de-Provence** clings to one of the highest ridges of the Alpilles. Lex Baux is divided into two: the bustling inhabited lower village, where elegant Renaissance houses line the shiny cobbled streets, and the deserted Ville Morte perched above, its ruined buildings hardly distinguishable from the surrounding limestone crags.

During the Middle Ages, this was the seat of the seigneurs de Baux, one of southern France's most powerful families. Their Cour d'Amour – a dazzling society of lords, ladies and wandering troubadours – was renowned throughout the Midi and, ever since, les Baux has been a romantic pilgrimage centre for poets and painters.

Picturesque Eygalières is hidden off the beaten track, surrounded by a wild, dusty landscape of olive and cypress trees. Its creamy stone houses, with sky blue and aquamarine shutters, line the lanes leading up to the village chapel (which now houses the **village museum**), a ruined castle and a spectacular panorama of the Alpilles. Try to visit during the first weekend of August, when this sleepy village hosts a merry fête and a splendid torchlit Arlésienne horseback parade.

AUBAGNE ✪

This old market town is now virtually a suburb of Marseille and yet, thanks to its thriving craft traditions, it has largely preserved its individual charm. Aubagne is well known for its pottery (particularly the small earthenware figures called *santons*w which originated here) and as the birthplace of the writer Marcel Pagnol. The films of his famous novels *Jean de Florette* and *Manon des Sources* have brought him to new prominence in recent years and admirers of his work can visit such sights as Manon's fountain and Pagnol's grave at la Treille by following clearly signed tours into the wild countryside that surrounds the town.

CASSIS ✪✪

This cheerful little fishing port and beach resort basks in a sheltered bay between the cliffs of the Cap Canaille, Europe's highest sea cliffs, and the breathtaking *calanques* to the west (➤ 16). The surrounding hills are smothered with olives, almonds, figs, and the famous terraced vineyards of the region's highly reputed white wine (➤ panel 94). In the village centre, *boccia* players meet in dusty squares while fishermen spread their nets along the bustling quayside, beside its colourful waterfront cafés. To explore the wondrous coastline, take a boat trip from a landing stage on the quay.

✚ 28B1
🛈 Tourist Office: quai des Moulins (☎ 04 42 01 71 17)
↔ Marseille (➤ 54), Aubagne (➤ 56)

STES-MARIES-DE-LA-MER ✪✪✪

The picture-postcard fishing village of Stes-Maries-de-la-Mer is steeped in the tradition and folklore of the Camargue (➤ 17), with its ancient whitewashed cottages, colourful costumes, bloodthirsty bull fights and flame-red sunsets. According to legend the Virgin Mary's half-sisters Maria Jacobé and Maria Salome landed here in AD 40 with their black serving maid Sarah, patroness of gypsies. When they died a chapel was built over their graves (later replaced by Notre-Dame-de-la-Mer) and the village has been a place of pilgrimage ever since.

The main pilgrimage takes place on 24–5 May. Gypsies, dressed in flounced skirts, brilliant shawls, ribbons and flowers, carry statues of the Marias and the bejewelled black Sarah in a small blue boat into the sea to be blessed, led by handsome mounted *gardiens* in full Camargue cowboy dress. There then follows a sparkling festival of bullfighting, rodoeos, flamenco and fireworks.

✚ 28A1
✉ Tourist Office: 5 avenue Van-Gogh (☎ 04 90 97 82 55)
↔ Arles (➤ 48)

A boat trip from Cassis is the best way to see the cliffs and coastline

57

28B2

ℹ️ Tourist Office: place Jean-Jaurès (☎ 04 90 92 05 22)

↔ Avignon (➤ 31), Cavaillon (➤ 41), Les Alpilles (➤ 56, 59), Tarascon (➤ 58)

Glanum

✉️ avenue Vincent van Gogh, Route des Baux

☎ 04 90 92 23 79

🕐 Apr–Sep, daily 9–7; Oct–Mar 10:30–5. Closed 1 Jan, 1 May, 11 Nov, 25 Dec

♿ Few

💵 Expensive

❓ Visits by guided tour (in French) only

 28A2

ℹ️ Tourist Office: 59 rue des Halles (☎ 04 90 91 03 52)

↔ Avignon (➤ 31); Arles (➤ 48), les Alpilles (➤ 56, 59), St Rémy-de-Provence (➤ 58)

Château de Tarascon

✉️ Boulevard de Roi-René

☎ 04 90 91 01 93

🕐 Oct–Mar, daily 10:30–6; Apr–Sep, daily 9–7. Closed 1 Jan, 1 May, 1, 11 Nov, 25 Dec

♿ Few

💵 Expensive

ST-RÉMY-DE-PROVENCE   ✪✪✪

Here you will find the true flavour of Provence – the warm peaches-and-cream coloured buildings, the maze of lanes, the fountains, the squares and the tree-lined boulevards. Nostradamus was born here in 1503, but today St-Rémy owes its popularity to van Gogh, who convalesced in an asylum just south of town after his quarrel with Gauguin and the ear-cutting incident in Arles. He produced 150 canvases and over 100 drawings during his one year's stay here, including *Starry Night*, *The Sower* and his famous *Irises*.

Near the asylum lie the extensive remains of the wealthy Greco-Roman town of **Glanum**, the oldest classical buildings in France. The area, covering about 2 hectares, was first settled in 6 BC and the city was abandoned in the 3rd century when it was overrun by barbarians. Buildings nearby, called Les Antiques, were also part of the Roman town: the oldest and smallest triumphal arch in France, dating from 20 BC and the best-preserved mausoleum of the Roman world, erected as a memorial to Caesar and Augustus.

TARASCON   ✪

Most people visit Tarascon, former frontier town of the kingdom of Provence, to see the Renaissance **fortress** of Good King René, with its moat and turreted towers on the banks of the Rhône. The town is also famous for its dreaded Tarasque, a man-eating monster who, according to legend, was vanquished by the town's patron, Sainte Marthe. On the last Sunday in June the green, dragon-like papier-mâché Tarasque parades around town, accompanied by Tartarin, a colourful character created by Alphonse Daudet, who mocks the *petite bourgeoisie* of Provence. This starts four days of fun with festivities, fireworks, bonfires and bullfights.

Rust-coloured rooftops, viewed from Good King Rene's fortress, Tarascon

A Drive from Arles round Les Alpilles to Tarascon

Head northwest out of Arles along the N570 then the D17 to the Abbey of Montmajour.

Once surrounded by marshes, this former Benedictine abbey is considered one of the most elaborate Romanesque churches in Provence.

Take the next turning right (D82), then over a crossroads, following signs to Aqueduc Romain.

These two ruined aquaducts once conveyed water from the Alpilles to Arles.

Back at the crossroads, turn right past the old windmill that inspired 19th-century novelist Alphonse Daudet to write his masterwork Lettres de mon Moulin *at Fontvieille. Leave town on the D17 through Paradou and continue to Maussane-les-Alpilles.*

Taste the wines of 14th-century Château d'Estoublon-Mogador just outside Fontvieille, or buy their prizewinning olive oil.

Remains of a Roman aquaduct that once supplied water to Arles

Once through Maussane, fork left on to the D78 following signs to le Destet and Eygalières (➤ 56). Exit Eygalières on the D74A. Turn left at the main road to St-Rémy-de-Provence (➤ 58). From here, take a small, unsignposted lane out of place de la République to St-Étienne-de-Grès.

St-Étienne is the hometown of the Provençal fabric manufacturer Olivades. Visit their factory here.

Continue on the D32 towards Arles to reach a busy junction beside a church.

The church is all that remains of the Gallo-Roman port of St-Gabriel, with one of the finest Romanesque façades in the Midi. The port flourished until the Middle Ages when the canal dried up.

Turn right at the junction, then take the D970 at the roundabout into Tarascon (➤ 58).

Distance
85km

Time
3¼ hours without stops; full day with visits

Start point
Arles
 28A2

End point
Tarascon
28A2

Lunch
Café des Arts, St-Rémy-de-Provence (➤ 95)
✉ 30 boulevard Victor-Hugo
☎ 04 90 92 08 50

In the Know

If you only have a short time to visit Provence and the Côte d'Azur, or would like to get a real flavour of the region, here are some ideas:

10
Ways to Be a Local

While away the hours in the local village bar.
Develop a taste for pastis.
Try your hand at *pétanque*.
Take a siesta.
Chat to locals about culinary delights, sport and politics.
Remember to address people as *monsieur*, *madame* or *mademoiselle*.
Sunbathe topless (but don't walk around town in beachwear afterwards)!
Relish the local cuisine.
Shop in local markets and sample the food before you buy.

Relax, unwind and settle into the Provençal pace of life.

10
Top Events

Aix International Festival of Music and Lyric Arts (Jul) – France's most elite music festival.
Arles *Féte des Gardians* (Apr) – Camarguais cowboys, *Arlésienne* girls, *farandole* dancing and bull-fights.
Avignon International Theatre Festival (Jul–Aug) – mainstream and fringe theatre.
Cannes International Film Festival (May, ► 85).

Châteauneuf-du-Pape Grape-ripening Festival (Aug) – troubadours, jousting, jugglers, banquets and free wine tasting.
Digne Lavender Festival (Aug) – Provence's most sweet-smelling festival.
Menton Lemon Festival (Feb) – spectacular procession of floats made out of 130 tonnes of golden citrus fruit.
Monaco Grand Prix (May) – Formula One in the streets of Monte-Carlo.
Nice Carnival (Feb) – the Riviera's biggest winter event.
Nice Jazz Festival (July) – Europe's leading open-air jazz festival, in an olive grove.

10
Top Activities

Take a helicopter from Nice Airport to Monte-Carlo (Héli Inter Riviera ☎ 04 93 21 46 46).
Go fishing and cook your catch on board (Sea Cruises Golfe-Juan ☎ 04 93 42 08 45).
Visit the Îles de Lérins (Compagnie Maritime Cannoise ☎ 04 93 38 66 33).
Hang-glide off the top of Mont Ventoux (Association Vaucluse Parapeute ☎ 04 90 85 67 82).

An elaborate display at Menton's Lemon Festival

Rehearsing for the bullfight in Arles

5
Top Markets

Aix-en-Provence (Flower Market – Tue, Thu, Sat am) – all the fragrance and colour of Provence.
Arles (Sat am) – an opportunity to see the Arlésienne women in traditional dress. Fruit, vegetables, soaps and fabrics, also saddles and stirrups.
Aubagne (Argilla) – biennial pottery market – the largest in France.
Marseille (Fish Market) – ad hoc boatside stalls.
Nice (cours Saleya) – voted one of France's most exceptional markets.

Take a boat trip to Corsica from Nice's old port (SNCM ☎ 04 93 13 66 66).
Ski Serre-Chevalier, Provence's largest ski resort (☎ 04 92 24 98 98).
Hire a Harley Davidson and cruise the streets of St-Tropez (Espace 83 ☎ 04 94 55 80 00).
Take the 'Pinecone Train' from Nice to Digne-les-Bains (☎ 04 97 03 80 80).
Canoe the Grand Cañon du Verdon (Aqua Viva Est ☎ 04 92 83 75 74).
Go horse riding in the Massif de l'Esterel or the Massif des Maures (Association Régionale du Tourisme Equestre ☎ 04 93 42 62 98).

5
Top Gardens

Cap Férat – Villa Ephrussi de Rothschild.
Monaco – Jardin Exotic.
Nice – Phoenix Parc Floral.
Entrecasteaux – château gardens.
Sérignan-du-Comtat – botanical herb garden.

Boating on the Grand Canyon du Verdon

5
Top Beaches

Cannes – best for star spotting.
Cassis (Calanques) – most scenic (▶ 16).
Iles d'Hyères (Plage de la Palud, Port-Cros) – best island beach.
Marseille (Plage du Prophète) – best water sports.
St-Tropez (La Voile Rouge) – the trendiest (▶ 66).

Var & Haute-Provence

No region of Provence displays such great diversity as the Var, the Alpes-de-Haute-Provence and the Hautes-Alpes. The Var boasts Provence's longest coastal strip, wild and rugged with deserted creeks and bleached beaches, far less developed than its famous Riviera neighbour. Its resorts are strung out like pearls along the coast, with St-Tropez the jewel in the crown. Inland, the Var is the most wooded region of France, with sombre green forests of chestnuts, cork oaks and conifers, interrupted only by an occasional yellow splash of mimosa or a quaint, hidden village.

By contrast, the two mountainous *départements* of Haute-Provence possess some of Provence's most sensational scenery, including Europe's 'Grand Canyon', the Gorges du Verdon. Picture-postcard villages and towns, rich in Provençal and Alpine architecture, bear witness to an eventful past, while the mountain air is filled with all the perfumes of Provence.

'If you would like to see the most beautiful land in the world, here it is'

PIERRE AUGUSTE RENOIR
(in a letter to Berthe Morisot)

The harbour at St-Tropez

St-Tropez

Even though the hedonistic image of St-Tropez in the Swinging Sixties has grown distinctly jaded, this charming little fishing port continues to seduce visitors and, despite being a tourist honey pot, remains a magnet for the rich and famous. In the words of the French writer Colette: 'Once you have visited here, you will never want to leave.'

Most visitors come to St-Tropez to rub shoulders with the glitterati in the waterfront cafés, and admire the grandiose yachts, moored before a backdrop of pink and yellow pastel buildings. These are relatively modern, recon-structed from original designs after the destruction that occurred during World War II. Take time to explore the narrow streets and medieval squares of old St-Tropez, where you will find a village of great character with its colourful markets, chic boutiques and romantic bistros.

Founded by Greeks as Athenopolis (City of Athena), the town has long been a popular meeting place for artists. Liszt and Maupassant were its first celebrities in the 1880s, followed by neo-Impressionist painter Signac a decade later. Soon Matisse, Bonnard, Utrillo and Dufy fell under St-Tropez' spell, immortalising the town in paint. Many pictures can

Mix with the rich and famous at Le Gorille – always an 'in' bar

be seen in the Musée de L'Annonciade (➤ 67).

An influx of writers arrived between the wars, including Colette, Cocteau and Anaïs Nin. Then in the 1950s it was the turn of the film stars, led by the famous Tropézienne, Brigitte Bardot. Her scandalous film, *Et Dieu Créa La Femme (And God Created Woman)* of 1956, marked the start of a permissive era and the Bardot/St-Tropez cult.

St-Tropez' star-studded list of residents includes Elton John, George Michael, Jean-Paul Belmondo and Jean Michel Jarre and, although it may no longer be how it was in its heyday, everything here is still extravagant, decadent, excessive. Little wonder the French endearingly call it St 'Trop' ('too much').

A Walk around St-Tropez

Start on the waterfront. Beside the Tourist Office, go through the Porte de la Poissonnerie, past the marble slabs of the daily fish market into place aux Herbes.

A stone's throw from the glamour of the quayside, the colourful daily fish, fruit and vegetable stalls remind visitors of St-Tropez' modest village past.

Leave the square up the steps of rue du Marché, turn left into rue des Commerçants, first right into rue du Clocher to Église St-Tropez (➤ 66). Continue along rue Cdt-Guichard to place de la Mairie, dominated by its handsome pink and green town hall, and place Garrezio.

The massive tower here is all that remains of St-Tropez' oldest building, 10th-century Château de Suffren, once home of the great 18th-century seaman, Admiral Suffren.

Return past the town hall and along rue de la Ponche. The 15th-century Porche de la Ponche archways lead to the old Ponche quarter.

This is the old fishing district of St-Tropez, centred on the sun-baked place du Revelin, overlooking the unspoiled fishing port and tiny shingle beach.

Head up rue des Ramparts, right at rue d'Aumale to the delightful place de l'Ormeau, and left up rue de l'Ormeau to rue de la Citadelle. Proceed downhill towards the port, taking the first left into rue Portail Neuf as far as the chapel.

The Chapelle de la Miséricorde with its quaint bell tower dates from the 17th century and the road alongside passes through its flying buttresses. The chapel's entrance is on rue Gambetta.

Continue along rue Gambetta for lunch in place des Lices (➤ 67).

Distance
1½km

Time
1–1½ hours, depending on church visits.

Start point
Waterfront

End point
Place des Lices

Lunch
Café des Arts (€) (➤ 97)
✉ Place des Lices
☎ 04 94 97 02 25

It's not all multi-millionaire's yachts at St-Tropez

65

Montée de la Citadelle
☎ 04 94 97 59 43
🕐 Apr–Sep 10–12:30,
1:30–6:30; Oct–Mar
10–12:30, 1:30–5:30.
Closed Tue, 2 Nov
♿ Few
💰 Moderate

 Rue de l'Église
🕐 Daily
↔ Vieux Port (➤ 67)

St-Tropez Beaches
Le Club 55
✉ Boulevard Patch
☎ 04 94 55 55 55

Tahiti-Plage
✉ Route de Tahiti
☎ 04 94 97 18 02

La Voile Rouge
✉ Route des Tamaris
☎ 04 94 79 84 34

What to See in St-Tropez

LA CITADELLE ✪✪
Visit this 16th-century hilltop fortress if only for the view, which embraces the orange curly-tiled roofs of St-Tropez' *vieille ville*, the dark and distant Maures and Esterel hills, and the glittering blue of the bay, flecked with sails. The Citadelle contains a naval museum, illustrating the town's long and glorious history, right up to the 1944 Allied landings that destroyed so much of the town.

ÉGLISE ST-TROPEZ ✪
St-Tropez owes its name to a Roman centurion called Torpes, who was martyred under Nero in AD 68. His head was buried in Pisa and his body put in a boat with a dog and cockerel who were to devour it. However, when the boat washed up here, his remains were miraculously untouched. For over 400 years the town's most important festival – the Bravade de St-Torpes (➤ 116) – has been celebrated in his honour. You can see a gilt bust of St Torpes and a model of his boat in the 19th-century baroque-style church, with its distinctive pink and yellow bell-tower.

Did you know ?

It was at the gorgeous sandy beaches of surrounding St-Tropez that girls first dared to bathe topless in the 1960s. In total, there are over 6km of enticing golden sand, neatly divided into invidual beaches, each with a different character, including trendy Club 55, which caters for the Paris set. Tahiti- Plage was once the movie stars' favourite, but nowadays star-spotters have more luck at the frivolous La Voile Rouge.

MUSÉE DE L'ANNONCIADE ✪✪✪

This former 16th-century chapel houses one of the finest collections of French late 19th-and early 20th-century paintings and bronzes. St-Tropez was then one of the most active centres of avant-garde art and, as a result, most of the 100 or so canvases here belong to the great movements of pointillism, fauvism and nabism. Many of the paintings portray local scenes. Look for Paul Signac's *L'Orage* (1895), Bonnard's *Le Port de St-Tropez* (1899), Camoin's *La Place des Lices* (1925), works by Dufy, Derain, Vuillard and others – and the museum cat, called Matisse!

✉ Place Georges-Grammont
☎ 04 94 97 04 01
🕐 Jun–Sep, Wed–Mon 10–12, 3–7; Oct–May, 10–12, 2–6. Closed 1 Jan, 1 May, Ascension, 25 Dec
♿ Few
✋ Moderate
↔ Vieux Port (► below)

PLACE DES LICES ✪✪

This is the real heart of St-Tropez, and remains very much as it looked in Camoin's 1925 *La Place des Lices* (► above), lined with ancient plane trees and bohemian cafés. The best time to visit is on Tuesdays or Saturdays for its colourful market, but come anytime for a game of boules and a glass of pastis with the locals.

✉ Place des Lices
🍴 Café des Arts (► 65)
♿ Good
❓ Shuttle buses to the beaches in summer

VIEUX PORT ✪✪✪

Artists and writers have been enticed to the pretty pastel-painted houses and crowded cafés which line the quay for over a century. Today, the waterfront is very much the place to see and be seen in St-Tropez, so try to arrive in your Aston Martin, on your Harley Davidson, or better still in an enormous floating gin palace, and remember to moor stern-to, giving onlookers a good view! It's such fun to wander along the quayside, to marvel at the size and cost of these ostentatious yachts and to watch their millionaire owners tucking into langoustines on deck, flamboyantly served by white-frocked crew.

✉ Vieux Port
🍴 Harbourfront bars, cafés and restaurants
♿ Good
↔ Musée de l'Annonciade (► above), Walk (► 65), Eglise de St-Tropez (► 66)

Two places to be seen: the beach; and the pastel-coloured waterfront

67

What to See in Var

AUPS ⭐⭐

69B2
Tourist Office: place Frédéric-Mistral (☎ 04 94 84 00 69)
Grand Cañon du Verdon (➤ 20), Moustiers-Ste-Marie (➤ 74)

The peaceful walled village of Aups basks in a wide valley, backed by undulating hills smothered in vines and olives, its name deriving from the Celto-Ligurian *alb* (hill pasture). The village enjoys a local reputation for its wine, honey, oil, black truffles and other regional specialities sold at the local Thursday-morning market. With its friendly folk, medieval gateways, shady streets, small squares dotted with fountains and a charming little museum of modern art in an old converted convent, Aups offers the perfect getaway from the well-trodden tourist tracks of Provence.

BORMES-LES-MIMOSAS ⭐⭐

69B1
Tourist Office: 9 place Gambetta (☎ 04 94 71 15 17)
Collobrières (➤ 70)

Despite a chequered history – founded by the Gauls, conquered by the Romans, then variously sacked by Saracens, Corsairs, Moors, Genoese and finally during the Wars of Religion – this hillside village remains one of the prettiest of the entire coast. Its ice-cream coloured pantiled houses spiral down steep stairways and alleys, with amusing names – Lover's Lane (Venelle des Amoreux),

Gossipers Way (Draille des Bredovilles) and steepest of all, Bottom-Breaker Road (Roumpi-Cuou)! Depending on the season, Bormes is bathed in the scent of mimosa, eucalyptus, oleander and camomile. In February, when the mimosa is in full bloom, it celebrates with its sensational *corso fleuri* – an extravaganza of floral floats made from myriads of tiny yellow flowers.

A *circuit touristique* embraces most of the sights including a fine 16th-century chapel dedicated to St François-de-Paule, an 18th-century church built in Romanesque style, a museum of local art, countless craft shops and a ruined fortress, affording dazzling sea views to the Îles d'Or (➤ 71) and inland over the Massif des Maures (➤ 70).

The circuit touristique *is a riot of flowers throughout the year*

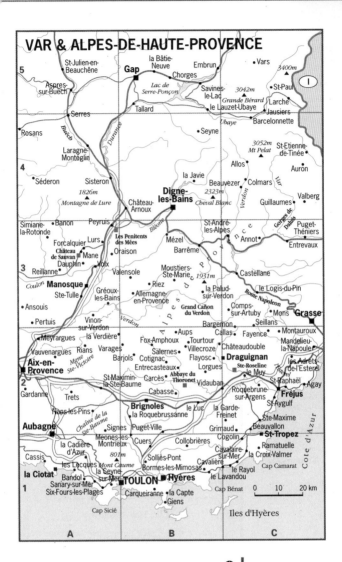

VAR & ALPES-DE-HAUTE-PROVENCE

St-Julien-en-Beauchêne · **Gap** · la Bâtie-Neuve · Chorges · Embrun · Vars · 3400m · St-Paul

Aspres-sur-Buëch · *Lac de Serre-Ponçon* · Savines-le-Lac · 3042m · le Lauzet-Ubaye · Jausiers · Larche · St-Paul

Grande Bérard

Serres · Tallard · *Ubaye* · Barcelonnette

Rosans · · Seyne

Laragne-Montéglin · 3052m · St-Etienne-de-Tinée · Mt Pelat

Séderon · Sisteron · la Javie · Allos · Auron

1826m · Château-Arnoux · Beauvezer · Colmars · Valberg

Montagne de Lure · **Digne-les-Bains** · 2323m · Guillaumes

Simiane-la-Rotonde · Banon · Peyruis · *Bléone* · St-André-les-Alpes · Puget-Théniers

Forcalquier · Les Pénitents des Mées · Mézel · Annot · Entrevaux

Château de Sauvan · Lurs · Mane · Oraison · Barrême · Route Napoléon

Reillanne · Dauphin · Volx · Moustiers-Ste-Marie · 1931m · Castellane

Manosque · Valensole · · le Logis-du-Pin

Ste-Tulle · Gréoux-les-Bains · Riez · la Palud-sur-Verdon · Comps-sur-Artuby · Mons · **Grasse**

Ansouis · Allemagne-en-Provence · Grand Cañon du Verdon · Bargemon · Seillans

Pertuis · Vinon-sur-Verdon · *Verdon* · · Montauroux

Meyrargues · la Verdière · Aups · Callas · Fayence · Mandelieu-la-Napoule

Vauvenargues · Rians · Varages · Fox-Amphoux · Tourtour · Châteaudouble · les Adrets de l'Esterel

Aix-en-Provence · Barjols · Salernes · Villecroze · Flayosc · **Draguignan** · Agay

Gardanne · Trets · Cotignac · Lorgues · Ste-Roseline · le Muy · **Fréjus**

St-Maximin-la-Ste-Baume · Carcès · Abbaye du Thoronet · Vidauban · **St-Raphaël**

Nans-les-Pins · Cabasse · le Luc · Roquebrune-sur-Argens · St-Aygulf

Brignoles · la Roquebrussanne · la Garde-Freinet · **Ste-Maxime**

Aubagne · Signes · Puget-Ville · Grimaud · Beauvallon · **St-Tropez**

Cassis · la Cadière d'Azur · Méounes-les-Montrieux · Cuers · Collobrières · Cogolin · Ramatuelle

801m · Mont Caume · Solliès-Pont · Cavalaire-sur-Mer · la Croix-Valmer

la Ciotat · les Lecques · la Seyne-sur-Mer · Bormes-les-Mimosas · Cavalière · le Rayol · Cap Camarat

Bandol · **TOULON** · **HYÈRES** · le Lavandou

Sanary-sur-Mer · Six-Fours-les-Plages · Carqueiranne · la Capte · Giens · Cap Bénat

Cap Sicié · Cap Bénat · **Îles d'Hyères**

0   10   20 km

COGOLIN ⭐

Old Cogolin, with its brightly coloured medieval houses, narrow cobbled streets and peaceful hidden *placettes* (tiny squares) bursting with flowers, offers a welcome escape from the crowds of nearby St-Tropez. Cogolin's economy depends on the traditional crafts of making cane furniture, silk yarn, brier pipes, knotted wool carpets and above all, reeds for wind instruments, attracting musicians of international renown.

✚ 69C1

ℹ Tourist Office: place de la République (☎ 04 94 55 01 10)

↔ St-Tropez (➤ 64), Port-Grimaud (➤ 71)

69B1

Tourist Office: boulevard Charles-Caminat (☎ 04 94 48 08 00)

Bormes-les-Mimosas (► 68)

69C2

Cannes (► 85), Fréjus (► 70)

69C2

Tourist Office: 325 rue Jean-Jaurès (☎ 04 94 51 83 83)

St-Tropez (► 64), Cannes (► 85)

Arène Frèjus

☎ 04 94 51 34 31

Apr–Sep 10–1, 2:30–6:30; Oct–Mar, 10–12, 1:30–5:30. Closed Tue

Free

COLLOBRIÈRES ⚫⚫

The tranquil village of Collobrières lies alongside the Collobrier river at the heart of the wild Massif des Maures, surrounded by densely forested hillside of cork oaks and chestnut trees bearing fruits the size of tennis balls. Collobrières is reputed to have been first in France to learn about corkage from the Spanish in the Middle Ages and cork production is still the major industry in the village, together with *marrons glacés* and other sweet chestnut confectionery.

CORNICHE DE L'ESTEREL ⚫⚫⚫

In stark contrast to the over-developed resorts to the east, the 'golden' Corniche de l'Esterel coast remains the sole stretch of wild coast left between St-Raphaël and the Italian border: a ragged shoreline of startlingly red cliffs, tumbling into a bright blue sea from the craggy wilderness of the Massif de l'Esterel beyond, piercing the coast with minute inlets, secret coves and tiny deserted bays. A narrow road (N98) twists along the clifftop, dipping down through some of the coast's least pretentious resorts, including Miramar and Agay. Inland, the blood-red porphyry mountains of the Massif, for centuries the haunt of bandits, are smothered in brilliant green spruce, pine and scrub, and ignited by wild flowers in summer.

FRÉJUS ⚫

The oldest Roman city in Gaul, founded by Julius Caesar in 49 BC, the flourishing naval town of Fréjus (Forum Julii) lay on the Aurelian Way from Rome to Arles. The fragile 1st- to 2nd-century **Roman arena** and theatre are still used for bullfights and concerts, and the remarkable Provençal cathedral contains one of France's oldest baptistries, perfectly preserved and dating from the 4th or 5th century. Following the decline of the Roman Empire, the port lost its significance and eventually silted up, forming the sandy beaches of Fréjus-Plage, a modern resort that merges into St-Raphaël.

Did you know ?

Ever since the Romans used it to scent their baths, lavender (from the Latin lavare *'to wash') has been in demand for its sweet smell and soothing qualities. There are two main types of plant: wild mountain lavender, which produces the most precious essences sought after by the makers of great perfumes, and* lavendin, *a hybrid grown in lower plains, which yields great quantities of inferior essence used in soap and other such products.*

GRIMAUD

One of Provence's most photogenic *villages perchés*, Grimaud is crowned by a romantic 11th-century château belonging to the Grimaldi family, after whom the village is named. By contrast, Port-Grimaud on the coast is a modern mini-Venice of ice-cream coloured designer villas lining the quayside. Designed by François Spoerry in the 1960s, it is best viewed by water taxi (*coche d'eau*) or from the church tower.

HYÈRES

The oldest of the Côte d'Azur winter resorts, Hyères-les-Palmiers is so-called because of its important palm-growing industry. Its popularity in the early 19th century had faded by the end of the century because it is 4km inland and not actually on the newly fashionable seaside. Hyères' main attraction today lies not in the town, but 10km off the Var coast – the three beautiful islands of the Îles d'Hyères.

69C2
Port-Grimaud: 1 boulevard des Alziers; Grimaud (☎ 04 94 43 26 98)
St-Tropez (► 64), Cogolin (► 69)
Tourist train links Port-Grimaud to the hilltop village of Grimaud

Waterside mansions of Port-Grimaud, Provence's mini-Venice; below, Hyères

69B1
Tourist Office: avenue A Thomas (☎ 04 94 01 84 50)
Three to five sailings daily for the Îles d'Or from Port de la Tour-Fondue, Presqu'île de Giens (☎ 04 94 58 21 81)

What to See in Alpes-de-Haute-Provence

COLMARS ✪

The name Colmars stems from Roman times when a temple to the god Mars was erected on the hill (Collis Martis), which today forms the backdrop to this small fortified village. Hidden in a high wooded valley of the Haut-Verdon, amid the highest peaks of the Alpes-de-Haute-Provence, the wooden alpine chalets, with their sloping roofs and balconies crimsoned with geraniums, seem far removed from the stone *mas* of the Var. It is here that the kingdom of France once bordered Savoy, hence the impregnable walls and two massive medieval castles, which crown the village and guard the bridges at either end. The northern **Fort de Savoie** is the more imposing and contains a cultural centre where exhibtions are held in the summer.

DIGNE-LES-BAINS ✪✪

This genteel town and departmental capital, in the pre-Alps beside the Bléone river, lies on the Route Napoléon, used by the emperor after his escape from Elba. Its sheltered location, mild sunny climate, invigorating air and the thermal springs to the south of town have made it a renowned spa.

Its other major attraction is lavender. This aromatic plant has been renowned since the Middle Ages for its therapeutic qualities, and Digne is the lavender-growing capital of Provence. During the spectacular purple processions of the annual lavender festival (➤ 60), even the streets get doused with lavender water! There is a Route de la Lavande, which passes through Digne and takes in all the main lavender producing places in the area. Digne also marks the end of the 'Pinecone' line, an ancient train which runs through the beautiful mountain valleys to Nice four times a day.

ENTREVAUX ✪✪

Sleepy Entrevaux was once an important border defence between France and Savoy, heavily fortified in the 1690s by Vauban, Louis XIV's military architect. Enter the village across a drawbridge, through one of three gatehouses into a hotchpotch of typical Provençal medieval houses, surprisingly untouched by the proximity of the Alps. The steep zig-zagging path to the mighty citadel that tops the ensemble is well worth the climb for the views of the Haut-Var and the surrounding mountains beyond.

Sidebar (Colmars):

✚ 69C4

ℹ Tourist Office: Porte de Savoie (☎ 04 92 83 41 92)

↔ Entrevaux (➤ below)

Fort de Savoie

🕐 Summer: 2–6:30

♿ Few

💷 Expensive

Sidebar (Digne-les-Bains):

✚ 69B4

ℹ Tourist Office: Rond-Point du 11-Novembre 1918 (☎ 04 92 36 62 62)

🚂 'Pinecone' line, four trains a day to Nice (☎ 04 97 03 80 80 for times)

↔ Les Mées (➤ 74), Sisteron (➤ 75)

Sidebar (Entrevaux):

✚ 69C3

ℹ Tourist Office: Porte Royale (☎ 04 93 05 46 73)

↔ Colmars (➤ above)

❓ Tourist office open summer only. Guided visits to citadel in Jul and Aug, 9–12, 3–6

The picture-postcard village of Entrevaux

FORCALQUIER ✪

This old market town is situated on the Roman Via Domita, which linked the Alps with the Rhône delta. It takes its name from the limestone kilns (*furni calcarii*) which the Romans hewed into the hillside. During the Middle Ages it was a powerful town and seat of the counts of Provence. Count Raimond, famous for his revelry, managed to marry off his four daughters to kings. On one occasion all four kings visited Forcalquier simultaneously and the region was dubbed the 'land of the four queens'! The surrounding countryside is particularly lush and beautiful. According to the nearby **Observatory of Haute Provence**, it has the cleanest, clearest air of anywhere in France, and makes a good base to explore the *villages perchés* of Limans, Banon, Dauphin and Simiane-la-Rotonde.

GRAND CAÑON DU VERDON (► 20, TOP TEN)

GRÉOUX-LES-BAINS ✪

Europe's oldest spa town lies in a beautiful, lavender and thyme-scented valley above the Verdon river, making it a perfect excursion base for outdoor sports, especially walking, cycling and fishing. Try its warm sulphurous waters, used since Roman times, and still popular today for treating arthritis, rheumatism and respiratory problems.

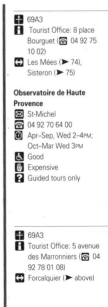

⊞ 69A3
🛈 Tourist Office: 8 place Bourguet (☎ 04 92 75 10 02)
↔ Les Mées (► 74), Sisteron (► 75)

Observatoire de Haute Provence
✉ St-Michel
☎ 04 92 70 64 00
🕐 Apr–Sep, Wed 2–4PM; Oct–Mar Wed 3PM
♿ Good
💷 Expensive
❓ Guided tours only

⊞ 69A3
🛈 Tourist Office: 5 avenue des Marronniers (☎ 04 92 78 01 08)
↔ Forcalquier (► above)

69B3
Tourist Office: rue de la Bourgade (mid-Jun to mid-Sep); Town Hall (rest of year) (☎ 04 92 74 67 84, 04 92 74 66 19)
Grand Cañon du Verdon (► 20), Aups (► 68)

MOUSTIERS-STE-MARIE ★★

Dramatically perched high on a ridge surrounded by sheer cliffs, Moustiers marks the start of the great gorges of the Verdon river (► 20). In the 17th and 18th centuries its white decorated earthenware pottery was famous throughout the world. Now *Faïence de Moustiers* has been revived and is sold in countless craft shops in every cobbled square.

The 5th-century chapel of Notre-Dame-de-Beauvoir is pinned against the rockface at the top of the village. Above it hangs a renowned gold star, suspended on a 227m chain, presented to the village by a knight called Blacas to celebrate his release from captivity during a crusade.

69B3
Information (☎ 04 92 34 36 38)
Digne-les-Bains (► 72), Sisteron (► 75)

LES PENITENTS DES MÉES ★

An extraordinary feature marks the entry into the Durance valley from Digne and the Provençal Alps – curiously eroded limestone pinnacles, which stand tightly packed together and tower 150m above the village of Les Mées (named after the Latin *metae*, milestone). According to a 5th-century legend local monks were attracted to some beautiful Moorish girls, captured by a knight during the Saracen invasions. Disgraced, they were banished from the village and, in punishment, turned to stone!

The best buy in Moustiers is undoubtedly its famous white faience

What to See in Hautes-Alpes

BRIANÇON ✪✪

This fortified city stands proudly amid the lofty snow-capped peaks of the southern Alps, and combines a rich historical past with an easy-going Provençal lifestyle. In summer the surrounding countryside is a hikers' paradise, and in winter Serre-Chevalier, one of France's top ski resorts, provides 250km of challenging ski slopes (➤ panel 110).

✚ Off map
ℹ Tourist Office: 1 place Temple (☎ 04 92 21 08 50)

EMBRUN ✪

Gateway to the wilderness of the Queyras and the lofty peaks of the Ecrins mountains, this colourful town was once an important episcopal seat. Make sure you see its former cathedral, one of the finest churches in the French Alps, boasting beautiful Renaissance stained glass and one of the oldest organs in France.

✚ 69B5
ℹ Tourist Office: 3 avenue Ernest Cézanne (☎ 04 92 43 72 72)

GAP ✪

This lively town and capital of the Hautes-Alpes, between Provence and the mountains of the Dauphiné, is popular for both summer and winter sports.

✚ 69B5
ℹ Tourist Office: 2a cours Frederic Mistral (☎ 04 92 52 56 56)

LA GRAVE ✪✪

One of the oldest and most important mountaineering stations in France, located on the northern edge of the Hautes-Alpes, opposite the imposing peak of la Meije (3,983m) – a great alpine challenge for climbers, a depressing number of whom are buried in its churchyard.

✚ Off map
ℹ Tourist Office, RN91 (☎ 04 76 79 90 05)

ST-VÉRAN ✪✪

The highest village in Europe at 2,040m, St-Véran consists of a handful of wooden chalets dotted over a mountainside near the Italian border. A track leads up through pastures sprinkled with anemones, gentians and other mountain flowers to the tiny chapel of Notre-Dame-de-Clausis, object of a pilgrimage from France and Italy every July.

✚ Off map
ℹ Tourist Office (☎ 04 92 45 82 21)

SISTERON ✪

Henri IV described the grandiose **citadel** of Sisteron (12th–16th century) as 'the most powerful fortress in my kingdom'. High on a rocky bluff, it dominates an unusually varied landscape, with the harsh Dauphiné mountains to the north and a rich valley to the south. The strategic importance of the town was emphasised as recently as 1944 when it suffered Allied air attacks. The citadel's guardroom contains a museum of local wartime resistance.

✚ 69A4
ℹ Tourist Office: place de la République (☎ 04 92 61 12 03)

La Citadelle
☎ 04 92 61 27 57
🕐 Daily 9–5:30 (7:30 Jul, Aug). Closed Nov–Mar
♿ Few 💰 Moderate **75**

Alpes-Maritimes

This dramatic stretch of vivid blue coastline with its chic cities, sandy beaches, craggy corniches and fishing villages has long attracted a rich assortment of actors, artists, writers and royalty to its shores. The luxury high-rise hotels, designer shops and terrace cafés of the smartest Riviera resorts – Cannes, Nice and Monaco – exude a carefree *joie de vivre*, basking in the scorching Mediterranean sun, while their ports overflow with millionaires' yachts. After all, this is the home of the rich and famous – the world's most sophisticated holiday playground.

If it weren't for the steep cliffs that plunge down to the sea between Nice and Menton it would be easy to forget that 80 per cent Alpes-Maritimes is composed of mountains. This is a region of wild, unexplored landscapes, whose slumbering villages – Biot, Saorge, St-Paul-de-Vence – offer visitors a chance to sample the true *douceur de vivre* of rural Provence.

'Thirst for the sun!
Thirst for the sand!
Thirst for the clocks that
run slow!'

JACQUES-HENRI LARTIGUE

Luxury yachts line a marina in Monaco

+ 83B2
ℹ Tourist Office: 5
promenade des Anglais
(☎ 08 92 70 74 07)

Nice

Nice is capital of the Alpes-Maritimes *département*, the Riviera's largest and most interesting city and France's largest tourist resort. Yet despite its status it remains a friendly place, full of Mediterranean character, with its own dialect (*lenga nissarda*), its own delicious cuisine (➤ 36–7) and a unique past.

A shipboard view of Nice, from the old port

Nice was originally founded by the Greeks in the 4th century BC. Then the Romans had a settlement at Cimiez, later ruined by Saracens. Nice began to thrive again in the Middle Ages, first under the counts of Provence, then under the Italian dukes of Savoy. Only unified with France in 1860, it retains a strong Italianate character, combining Italian temperament and lifestyle with French finesse and savoir faire.

Thanks mainly to the British, by the 1860s Nice was already Europe's most fashionable winter retreat, and exuberant *belle-époque* hotels sprang up along the fashionable palm-lined waterfront, aptly named the promenade des Anglais. Nearby, the alleyways and markets of the *vieille ville* contrast boldly with the broad boulevards and designer shops of the modern city around the handsome main square, place Masséna. The entire city is cradled by the vineclad foothills of the maritime Alps.

This delightful setting has attracted many artists over the years. As a result, Nice is blessed with more museums and galleries than any French town outside Paris.

A Walk around Nice Vieille Ville

Start at the western end of cours Saleya.

This square is where Nice's famous outdoor flower, fruit and vegetable market is held (▶ 81), an ideal place to hear the local patois and to taste *socca, pissaladière* and other local delicacies.

Head east past the palace of the former dukes of Savoy and the Italianate 18th-century Chapelle de la Misericorde to the yellow house at the end of the square, where Matisse once lived. Turn left into rue Gilly then continue along rue Droite, past Palais Lescaris.

Rue Droite contains some of the old town's top galleries and Provence's best bread shops (Espuno ▶ 107). Palais Lascaris, an ornate 17th-century Genoese-style mansion, houses the Musée des Arts-et-Traditions-Populaires, containing sumptuous period paintings, furnishings and *trompe l'oeil* ceilings.

Continue straight on until place St–François and the early morning fish market.

Unusually, this is an *inland* fish market but, before the Paillon river was filled in, fishermen used to land here to sell their catch.

Continue down rue St–Francois. Bear right into rue du Collet, left at place Centrale along rue Centrale, then right into rue Mascoïnat until you reach place Rossetti.

Place Rossetti is dominated by the beautiful Baroque Cathédrale Ste-Réparate, with its emerald dome of Niçoise tiles. Enjoy a coffee in one of the cafés here or an ice cream from Fenocchio's (▶ 99).

Leave the square along rue Ste-Reparate. At the end, turn right into rue de la Prefecture.

The great violinist Niccolò Paganini lived and died at No 23.

A right turn opposite Paganini's house into rue St-Gaètan takes you back to cours Saleya.

The colours of old Nice – sunny terracotta and cool green shutters

Distance
2km

Time
1–2 hours, depending on shopping, museum and church visits

Start/end point
Cours Saleya
🚌 All buses

Lunch
Chez Freddy (€€)
✉ 22 cours Saleya
☎ 04 93 85 49 99

It comes as a surprise to find a Russian church in Nice

What to See in Nice

CATHÉDRALE ORTHODOXE RUSSE ST-NICOLAS ⭐

This magnificent pink and grey Russian Orthodox church, crowned by six gleaming green onion-shaped cuppolas, was built by Tzar Nicolas II in 1903 in memory of his son Nicolas, who is buried in the grounds. Brimming with precious icons, frescoes and treasures, the church still conducts regular services in Russian.

✉ Avenue Nicolas-II
☎ 04 93 96 88 02
🕐 Daily 9:15–12, 2:30–6 (5:30 winter). Closed Sun AM
🚌 5,7,17,23,24
♿ Good 🏷 Cheap

CIMIEZ ⭐⭐

Nice's smartest residential area owes much of its original cachet to Queen Victoria who used to winter here at the once-palatial Hotel Regina. Nearby lies an excavated Roman settlement, a small **archaeological museum**, and a 16th-century Franciscan Monastery and Church, containing three masterpieces by Nice-born primitive painter Louis Bréa. Dufy and Matisse lie buried in the adjacent cemetery. Europe's leading international Jazz Festival is held in Cimiez every July, in the beautiful olive grove beside the Musée Matisse.

Musée Archéologique de Cimiez
✉ 160 avenue des Arènes
☎ 04 93 81 59 57
🕐 10–6. Closed Tue
🚌 15,17, 20, 22, 25
♿ Few 🏷 Moderate
❓ Guided tours by appointment

MUSÉE D'ART MODERNE ET D'ART CONTEMPORAIN (MAMAC) ⭐⭐⭐

The museum's collections trace the history of French and American avant-garde art from the 1960s to the present: new realists, American pop art, minimalism and the Nice School, in particular its founder Yves Klein. The building, itself a 'museum-monument', is a masterpiece of modern architecture with fine views from its rooftop terraces. On occasional late-night Fridays in summer the illumination of Klein's *Mur de Feu* (Wall of Fire) is a sight to behold.

✉ Promenade des Arts
☎ 04 93 62 61 62
🕐 Tue–Sun 10–6. Closed Mon and hols
🚌 3, 4, 5, 6, 7, 9, 16, 17, 25, 30
🍴 Cafés & restaurants (€€)
♿ Excellent 🏷 Moderate

MUSÉE MARC-CHAGALL (MESSAGE BIBLIQUE) ✪✪✪

Located in the heart of a Mediterranean garden, this striking modern museum was specially built to house Chagall's 'Biblical Message' – a series of 17 monumental canvases evoking the Garden of Eden, Moses and other Old Testament themes. The museum was opened by the artist himself in 1973. Chagall also made the mosaic and the beautiful blue stained-glass windows in the concert hall.

Other creations, including paintings, etchings, lithographs, sculptures and tapestries, were donated to the museum after Chagall's death in 1985, making this the most important permanent collection of his work.

⊠	Avenue Docteur-Ménard
☎	04 93 53 87 20
🕐	Jul–Sep, Wed–Mon 10–6; Oct–Jun, 10–5. Closed 1 Jan, 1 May, 25 Dec
🍴	Garden café Apr–Oct (€)
🚌	15
♿	Excellent
💷	Moderate
↔	Cimiez (► 80)
❓	Shop, library, concert hall. Reserve guided tours in advance

The remarkable Chagall Museum is a must for all

MUSÉE MATISSE (► 22, TOP TEN)

PROMENADE DES ANGLAIS ✪✪

As its name suggests, this palm-lined promenade, which graciously sweeps round the Baie des Anges (Bay of Angels), was constructed at the expense of Nice's wealthy English residents in 1822 so they could stroll along the shoreline. Today it is bordered by a highway of *autoroute* proportions and the white wedding-cake style architecture of the luxury *belle-époque* hotels, such as the world-famous Negresco (► 103), are now juxtaposed with ugly concrete apartment blocks. Don't miss the **Musée Masséna**, next to the Negresco, devoted to regional history and including Napoleonic mementos (currently closed for renovation), or the remarkable collections of the nearby **Museum of Naive Art**.

Musée Masséna

⊠	35 promenade des Anglais
☎	04 93 88 11 34
🚌	3, 7, 9, 8, 10, 11. 12, 14, 22
❓	Closed for renovation until 2005

Musée d'Art Naif

⊠	Château Ste-Hélène, avenue du Val Marie
☎	04 93 71 78 33
🕐	Wed–Mon 10–6. Closed some hols
🚌	6, 9, 10, 12, 23, 24, 26, 34
♿	Few 💷 Moderate

VIEILLE VILLE AND COURS SALEYA ✪✪✪

Old Nice is a maze of dark narrow streets, festooned with flowers and laundry and brimming with cafés, hidden squares and bustling markets. Dismissed as a dangerous slum in the 1970s, this is now the trendiest part of Nice, lively day and night, especially cours Saleya. This spacious, sunny square is scene of one of France's top fruit and vegetable markets – the tastes, fragrances and colours of Provence and Italy are a feast for the senses. By night, cafés and restaurants fill the cours, making it one of Nice's most animated night spots.

| 🚌 | All buses |
| ❓ | Fruit and vegetable market Tue–Sun AM; flower market (all day except Sun PM); flea market Mon |

83B2

Tourist Office: 2a
boulevard des Moulins
(☎ 0377 92 16 61 16)

Cap Ferrat (➤ 86), the
Corniches (➤ 86), Èze
(➤ 87), Menton (➤ 88),
Nice (➤ 78), Saorge
(➤ 89), Villefranche-sur-
Mer (➤ 90)

Monaco

**After the Vatican, Monaco is the world's smallest
sovereign state, a 195-hectare spotlessly clean strip
of skyscraper-covered land squeezed between sea
and mountains. There are no taxes and the world's
highest incomes attract the rich and famous.**

Monaco is the name of the principality and also the district
on the peninsula to the south, containing the old town with

its narrow streets and pastel-coloured
houses, a startling contrast to the
newer high-rise district of Monte-
Carlo, centred round its glitzy casino
and designer shops. With so much
evident wealth and glamour it is hard
to imagine Monaco's turbulent past,
at various times occupied by the
French, the Spanish and the dukes of
Savoy. The present ruling king is
Prince Rainier III, whose family, the
Grimaldis, have ruled Monaco for 700
years – the world's oldest reigning
monarchy.

The Grimaldis once held sway over
an area that extended along the coast
and included Menton and
Roquebrune. However, their high
taxes provoked a revolt and the principality shrank to its present size.
Facing a financial crisis, Charles III of
Monaco decided to turn to gambling
for his revenue, not by betting the
royal reserves but by opening a
casino. Such was its success that
taxes were soon abolished altogether.

The ornate casino

What to See in Monaco

CASINO ●●●

Even if you are not a gambler, it is worth visiting the
world's most famous casino, designed in 1878 by Charles
Garnier, architect of the Paris Opéra, to see the opulent
belle-époque interior and tiny, highly ornate opera house,
the Salle Garnier, which has been graced by many of the
world's most distinguished opera singers. The dazzlingly
illuminated place du Casino by night is a must see. The
Café de Paris and Hôtel de Paris are worth a look too.

✉ Place du Casino

☎ 0377 92 16 20 20

🕐 European Rooms from
2PM; Private Rooms 4PM

❓ Over 18s only. Passport
required

🚌 1, 4, 6

♿ Good 💶 Expensive

THE CÔTE D'AZUR

Loup ▲1777m
St Martin-du-Var
Utelle
Col de Brouis 879m
Saorge
Roya
3
Gorges du Loup
Levens
Col de Braus 1002m
Breil-sur-Roya
St Martin-du-Var
L'Escarène
Sospel
Vence
Var
N85
St-Paul-de-Vence
A8/E80
I
Grasse
Cagnes-sur-Mer
Biot
Monte-Carlo
Menton
Mandelieu-la-Napoule
Mougins
Villefranche
NICE
MC
Roquebrune-Cap-Martin
Cap Ferrat
A8/E80
Antibes
Cap d'Antibes
2
Cannes
Juan-les-Pins
Le Trayas
Îles de Lérins
Côte d' A z u r
Côte   d'Azur
N
1
0   10   20   30 km

A   B   C

CATHÉDRALE ⭐

Built in 1875 (funded by casino profits), this ostentatious neo-Romanesque cathedral stands on the site of a 13th-century church dedicated to St Nicolas. Among its treasures are two 16th-century retables by Niçoise artist Louis Bréa and tombs of the former princes of Monaco and the much mourned Princess Grace.

MUSÉE OCÉANOGRAPHIQUE ⭐⭐⭐

Founded by Prince Albert I in 1910 to house his remarkable collections of marine flora, fauna, nautical instruments and a 20-m whale skeleton, this spectacular aquarium and museum of marine science is the finest of its kind in the world. It is located in a grandiose building on a sheer cliff high above the Mediterranean. Marine explorer Jacques Cousteau set up his research centre here and his remarkable films are regularly screened in the museum's cinema.

PALAIS DU PRINCE ⭐

In summer, when Prince Rainier is away, guided tours take visitors through the priceless treasures of the State Apartments and the small Musée Napoléon in the south wing of the palace. When he is in residence the royal colours are flown from the tower and visitors must content themselves with the Changing of the Guard ceremony (daily at 11:55AM).

- ⊠ 4 rue Colonel-Bellando-de-Castro
- ☎ 0377 93 30 87 70
- ⏰ Daily 7–7
- 🚌 1, 2
- ♿ Good
- ✋ Free

- ✚ 83B2
- ⊠ Avenue St-Martin
- ☎ 0377 93 15 36 00
- ⏰ Oct–Mar 10–6; Apr, May, Jun & Sep 9:30–7; Jul, Aug 9:30–7:30
- 🍴 Restaurant & bar
- 🚌 1, 2
- ♿ Good
- ✋ Very expensive

- ⊠ Place du Palais
- ☎ 0377 93 25 18 31
- ⏰ Jun–Sep, 9:30–6; Oct 10–5. Closed Nov–May
- 🚌 1, 2 ♿ Few
- ✋ Expensive
- ↔ Cathédrale

What to See in Alpes–Maritimes

ANTIBES ●●

Antibes was founded in the 5th century BC as a Greek trading post, and centuries later was controlled by the dukes of Savoy until the 18th century. Napoléon was held prisoner here in 1794 in Vauban's mighty 17th-century Fort Carré on the eastern edge of town. Today, its massive ramparts protect Old Antibes from flooding. The Grimaldi family ruled from the 12th- to 16th-century seafront château, which today houses one of the world's finest Picasso collections (➤ 23).

Old Antibes, which lies hidden behind the ramparts, is a maze of cobbled, winding lanes overflowing with shops, restaurants and bars. Don't miss the bustling morning market in cours Masséna or the craft market on Friday and Sunday afternoons (also Tuesdays and Thursdays in summer). On the waterfront, the Port Vauban yacht harbour boasts some of the Côte d'Azur's most luxurious yachts.

BIOT ●●●

Five kilometres north of Antibes lies the charming hilltop village of Biot – a mass of steep cobbled lanes lined with quaint sand-coloured houses capped by orange-tiled roofs, leading up to the famous arcaded main square. The streets are decorated with huge earthenware jars ablaze with geraniums and tropical plants, as, for centuries, Biot has been a thriving pottery centre. It is also known for its gold and silverwork, ceramics, olive-wood carving and thriving glassworks. Visitors can watch glass-blowers at the Verrerie de Biot demonstrating their unique *verre bullé* (bubble glass).

Near by, the striking **Musée Fernand-Léger**, with its huge brilliantly coloured mosaic façade and monumental stained-glass windows, was founded in 1959 in memory of cubist painter Fernand Léger who lived at Biot for a short time and inspired the growth of the craft workshops here. The museum contains nearly 400 of his works, including ceramics, tapestries, stained glass and mosaics.

CAGNES-SUR-MER ●●

Cagnes is divided into three: the old fishing quarter and main beach area of Cros-de-Cagnes; Cagnes-Ville, the commercial centre with its smart racecourse beside the sea; and Haut-de-Cagnes. This inviting hilltop village, with its brightly coloured houses smothered in bougainvillea, mimosa and geraniums, is crowned by a 14th-century château, built by Admiral Rainer Grimaldi as a pirate lookout. Renoir spent the last 11 years of his life nearby at Domaine des Collettes, now the **Musée Renoir**. He would sit and paint beneath the olive trees, his brushes strapped to his rheumatic fingers.

CANNES ✪

Think Cannes, think movies and film stars, expensive boutiques, palatial hotels and paparazzi! After all, it is one of the world's most chic resorts, twinned with Beverly Hills and, within France, second only to Paris for shopping, tourism and major international cultural and business events, including the world-famous film festival (➤ 116).

With so much glitz it is easy to forget that Cannes was a mere fishing village until 1834, when retired British chancellor Lord Brougham, en route to Nice, was enchanted by its warm climate and quaint setting and built a villa here to spend the winter months. Soon hundreds of other aristocrats and royals followed his example. Before long hotels began to spring up along the waterfront. However, it was not until the 1930s that Cannes became a summer resort, made fashionable by visiting Americans. By the 1950s mass summer tourism had taken off and has been the lifeblood of Cannes ever since.

The town is divided into two parts. The Vieux Port and old Roman town of Canois Castrum (now known as le Suquet) occupy a small hill to the west, crowned by an 11th-century castle and watchtower affording a sweeping coastal vista. To the east, modern Cannes is built round la Croisette, Europe's most elegant sea promenade, lined with palms and flanked by designer shops, grand *belle-époque* hotels and the sparkling Golfe de la Napoule with its golden beaches (of imported sand to cover the natural shingle), each with their tidy rows of coloured parasols and mattresses.

🔲 83A2

ℹ️ Tourist Office: Palais des Festivals, 1a Croissette (☎ 04 93 39 24 53)

↔️ Antibes (➤ 84); Biot (➤ 84); Mougins (➤ 89)

❓ International Film Festival in May (➤ 116). Cinemas screen films from early morning well into the night, but it is difficult to get tickets.

The Old Port – a reminder of Canne's origins as a humble fishing village

85

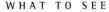

83B2

Tourist Office: 59 avenue Denis Semeria (☎ 04 93 76 08 90)

The Corniches (➤ below), Èze (➤ 87), Nice (➤ 78), Villefranche- sur-Mer (➤ 90)

Villa Ephrussi de Rothschild

✉ Chemin du Musée-St-Jean-Cap-Ferrat

☎ 04 93 01 33 09

🕐 10–6 (7 in summer). Closed 25 Dec

🍴 Salon de thé (€€)

♿ Few

💷 Very expensive

❓ Guided tours available

83B2

Nice (➤ 78), Monaco (➤ 82), Èze (➤ 87)

Opposite: *the Jardin Exotique at Èze*
Below: *Cary Grant and Grace Kelly on the corniches*

CAP-FERRAT ✪

The most desirable address on the Côte d'Azur – the 'Peninsula of Billionaires', with its huge villas hidden in subtropical gardens – has long been a favourite haunt of the rich and famous, including King Leopold II of Belgium, Somerset Maugham, Edith Piaf, the Duke and Duchess of Windsor, Charlie Chaplin and David Niven. A delightful coast path from Villefranche around the cape past countless tiny azure inlets (ideal for a refreshing dip), makes a pleasant stroll before lunch in the former fishing village of St-Jean-Cap-Ferrat.

Cap-Ferrat's finest villa – considered by many the finest on the Riviera – is the **Villa Ephrussi de Rothschild**, a rose-pink *belle-époque* palace constructed by the flamboyant Baroness Béatrice Ephrussi de Rothschild (1864–1934), set in immaculate formal gardens with wonderful sea views. The remarkable interior is lavishly decorated with rare furniture (including some pieces that once belonged to Marie Antoinette), set off by rich carpets, tapestries and an eclectic collection of rare objets d'art.

THE CORNICHES ✪✪✪

Three famous corniches (cliff roads) traverse the most scenic and most mountainous stretch of the Côte d'Azur from Nice to Menton via Monaco. Called La Grande (D2564), La Moyenne (N7) and L'Inférieure, they each zig-zag their way along vertiginous ledges at three different elevations. La Grande Corniche, at the highest level, was first constructed by Napoléon and is by far the best choice for picnickers and lovers of plants and wildlife.

The lowest route (Corniche Inférieure) follows the coastal contours through all the seaside resorts, and is best avoided in the main tourist season of July and August.

The steep Corniche Moyenne in the middle is undoubtedly the most dramatic – a cliff-hanging route with hair-raising bends, sudden tunnels and astounding views, frequently used for car commercials and movie car chases.

ÈZE ✪✪✪

Èze, the most strikingly situated and best-preserved Provençal *village perché*, stands high on a rocky pinnacle ten minutes' drive from Nice and Monaco. Frequently called the *Nid d'Aigle* (Eagle's Nest), it boasts frequent views over the entire Riviera as far as Corsica.

Tall, golden stone houses and a labyrinth of tiny vaulted passages and stairways climb steeply up to the ruins of the once-massive Saracen fortress 429m above sea level, surrounded by an **exotic garden**, bristling with magnificent cacti, succulents and rare palms. Take time to explore the countless craft shops housed in small caves within the rock – tiny treasure troves of antiques, ceramics, pewter and olive-wood carvings. At the foot of the hill, the two perfume factories of Galimard and Fragonard both contain fascinating museums.

✚ Off map
ℹ Tourist Office: place de Gaulle (☎ 04 93 41 26 00)
↔ Cap-Ferrat (➤ 86), The Corniches (➤ 86), Menton (➤ 88), Monaco (➤ 82), Nice (➤ 78), Villefranche-sur-Mer (➤ 90)

Jardin Exotique
✉ Rue du Château
☎ 04 93 41 10 30
🕐 9–6:30 (8 Jul, Aug)
♿ None
💰 Moderate

GRASSE ✪✪

For 400 years Grasse has been the capital of the perfume industry. Until recently 85 per cent of the world's flower essence was created here, and this sleepy, fragrance-filled town is still France's leading centre for the cut flower market. Learn about the history and alchemy of the perfume industry at the Musée International de la Parfumerie, or take a guided tour around **Maison Fragonard**, Grasse's largest perfume factory, named after a local artist Jean-Honoré Fragonard (1732–1806). Or why not create your own personal fragrance at **Studio des Fragrances Galimard**?

🔲 83A3

ℹ️ Tourist Office: 3 place de la Foux (☎ 04 93 36 21 68) and Palais de Congrès (☎ 04 93 36 03 56 66)

🔁 Cannes (► 85), Mougins (► 89)

Maison Fragonard

✉️ 20 boulevard Fragonard

☎ 04 93 36 44 65

🕐 Daily 9–6:45

♿ Good

🎟️ Free

Studio des Fragrances Galimard

✉️ route de Pégomas

☎ 04 93 09 20 00

🕐 Daily by appointment. Allow 2 hours

♿ Good

🎟️ Free, but very expensive to create your own perfume

Grasse perfume bottles

Did you know?

Grasse was originally a tannery town, where, in the 16th century, Italian glove makers began to use local flowers to perfume leather gloves, a fashion made popular by Catherine de' Medici. Acre upon acre of lavender, mimosa, roses, jasmine and jonquils were cultivated and Grasse soon became the centre of the French perfume industry, creating the essences for Chanel, Givenchy and many other famous brands.

MENTON ✪✪

Just 1.6km from the border, France's most Italianate resort, with its steep jumble of tall, honey-coloured houses, is wedged between a sweeping palm-lined bay and a dramatic mountain backdrop. Menton is France's warmest town, boasting an annual 300 days of sun and resulting in a town bursting with semi-tropical gardens. Menton is also the 'lemon capital of the world', smothered in citrus groves. Every February a spectacular Lemon Festival takes place in the Jardins Biovès (► 60).

Make sure you see the medieval old town, with its two magnificent ice-cream coloured churches – Église St-

🔲 83C2

ℹ️ Tourist Office: Palais de l'Europe, avenue Boyer (☎ 04 92 41 76 76)

🔁 Èze (► 87), Monaco (► 82), Saorge (► 89)

Michel and the Chapelle de la Conception – and the beautiful old cemetery beyond with its striking sea views. Other notable sights include the Musé Jean-Cocteau, the Musée de la Préhistoire Régional, boasting the remains of 'Menton Man' (30,000 BC), and Palais Carnolès, the sumptuous 18th-century summer residence of the princes of Monaco, now Menton's main art museum.

Menton's proximity to Italy is apparent in its architecture (and abundance of pasta restaurants)

MOUGINS ✪✪

At first glance Mougins appears a typical Provençal hill village, but inside its medieval walls lies one of the Riviera's smartest villages. Past residents include Jacques Brel, Yves Saint Laurent, Catherine Deneuve, and Picasso, whose photos are displayed in the **Musée de la Photographie**.

The real attraction, however, is the sheer volume of top restaurants. Try Les Muscadins (► 99) or La Ferme de Mougins. For a real treat, Le Moulin de Mougins (► 98) just outside the village is considered one of the most prestigious in the world.

✚ 83A2
ℹ Tourist Office: 15 avenue Charles-Mallet (☎ 04 93 75 87 67)

Musée de la Photographie
✉ Porte Sarrazine
☎ 04 93 75 85 67
◷ Wed–Sat 10–12, 2–6; Sun 10–2. Closed Mon, Tue. Jul–Sep daily 10–8
♿ Few
💷 Cheap

SAORGE ✪

As you climb the panoramic Roya valley into the mountains from the coast, the medieval village of Saorge is a magnificent sight. Hanging 200m above the river, its tidy rows of Italian slate-roofed, ochre and blue houses rise in tiers, in the typical style of a *village empilé* (stacked village). Once a Piedmontese border stronghold, Saorge was taken by the French in 1794 but has still retained its unique customs and dialect. Outside the village, the elegant baroque **Franciscan monastery** offers precipitous views into the valley.

✚ 83C3
ℹ la Mairie (☎ 04 93 04 51 23)
↔ Menton (► 88); Monaco (► 82)

Couvent des Franciscains
☎ 04 93 04 55 55
◷ Wed–Mon 2–6

ST-PAUL-DE-VENCE ✪✪✪

Gently draped over a hill close to Cagnes, this picture-postcard *village perché* was appointed a 'Royal Town' in the 16th century by King François. Today it is a tourist honeypot, with coachloads flocking to the Fondation Maeght (► 18) and the smart shops and galleries. Yet despite the crowds it remains one of Provence's most beautiful villages, especially at night when the narrow alleys are lit with tiny lanterns.

✚ 83A3
ℹ Tourist Office: Maison de la Tour, 2 rue Grande (☎ 04 93 32 86 95)
↔ Antibes (► 84), Biot (► 84), Cagnes (► 84), Nice (► 78), Vence (► 90)

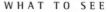

★ 83A3

ℹ Tourist Office: place du Grand-Jardin (☎ 04 93 58 06 38)

↔ Antibes (►84), Biot (►84), Cagnes (►84), Nice (►78), St-Paul-de-Vence(►89)

Chapelle du Rosaire

✉ Avenue Henri-Matisse

☎ 04 93 58 03 26

⏰ Mon, Wed, Sat 2–5:30, Tue, Thu 10–11:30, 2–5:30 (Fri 2–5:30 during school hols). Sun 10:45–11:30. Closed Fri & Nov

♿ Good **💲** Cheap

The serenity of the Chapelle du Rosaire is reflected in Matisse's minimalist drawings

VENCE ●●

This delightful old town, only 10km inland from the coast, was once the Roman forum of Vintium. In the Middle Ages it became a bishopric, and its 10th-century cathedral (the smallest in France) is rich in treasures, including Roman tombstones embedded in the walls and a remarkable Chagall mosaic.

Vence has long attracted artists and, in 1941, Henri Matisse moved here to escape Allied bombing on the coast, but he then fell seriously ill. Dominican sisters nursed him back to health and, as a gift, he built and decorated the tiny **Chapelle du Rosaire** for them. The interior is compelling in its simplicity, with powerful black line drawings of the Stations of the Cross on white faience, coloured only by pools of yellow, blue and green light from the enormous stained-glass windows. Matisse worked on this masterpiece well into his 80s, considering it his 'ultimate goal, the culmination of an intense, sincere and difficult endeavour'.

★ 83B2

ℹ Tourist Office: Jardin François-Binon (☎ 04 93 01 73 68)

↔ Cap-Ferrat (►86), the Corniches (►86), Èze (►87)

Chapelle St-Pierre

✉ quai Courbet, Port de Villefranche

☎ 04 93 76 90 70

⏰ Tue–Sun 9:30–12, 3–7

♿ Good **💲** Moderate

VILLEFRANCHE-SUR-MER ●●

Considering its proximity to Nice and Monte-Carlo, Villefranche remains surprisingly unspoilt, little changed since it was founded in the 14th century as a customs-free port (hence its name). Its picturesque natural harbour is fringed with old red and orange Italianate houses, tempting waterfront bars, cafés and restaurants.

Take time to explore the maze of steep stairways and cavernous vaulted passageways which climb from the harbour through the *vieille ville*, and the sturdy 16th-century citadel, with galleries of paintings and sculptures by local artists, including Picasso and Mirò. By the quay, the tiny 14th-century **Chapelle St-Pierre**, once used to store fishing nets, was decorated in 1957 with frescoes by Villefranche's most famous resident, Jean Cocteau.

Where To...

Above: santon *figurines
for sale*
Right: *Cannes Film Festival
sculpture*

Vaucluse

Opening Hours and Prices

Prices are approximate, based on a three-course meal for one without drinks and service:

€ = under €25
€€ = €25–50
€€€ = over €50

The restaurants on the following pages are all open for lunch and dinner daily unless otherwise stated.

A Meal In Provence

'By 12:30 the little stone-walled restaurant was full. There were some serious stomachs to be seen … The proprietor of the restaurant … quivered with enthusiasm as he rhapsodised over the menu: foie gras, lobster mousse, beef *en croûte*, salads dressed in virgin oil, hand-picked cheeses, desserts of a miraculous lightness, *digestifs*. It was a gastronomic aria which he performed at each table.'

(*A Year in Provence* by Peter Mayle)

Avignon

Le Belgocargo (€)
Belgian restaurant offering 16 types of *moules frites* on a huge sunny terrace.
✉ 10 place des Châtaignes
☎ 04 90 85 72 99 🕐 12–2, 7–10:30. Closed Sun, except Jul, Aug

Christian Étienne (€€€)
One of Avignon's gourmet temples in a 14th-century palace beside the Palais des Papes. Try the fish, foie gras and truffle specialities.
✉ 10 rue de Mons ☎ 04 90 86 16 50 🕐 Closed Sun & Mon

Le Cloître (€)
Savoury or sweet pancakes washed down with a bowl of cider, in a cosy traditional restaurant.
✉ 9 place du Cloître-St-Pierre ☎ 04 90 85 34 63 🕐 Tue–Sat 12–2:30, 7–midnight

La Fourchette (€€)
A smaller, more relaxed, cheaper offspring of Hiély-Lucullus (► below), nonetheless with delicious dishes. Very popular. Reservations essential.
✉ 17 rue Racine ☎ 04 90 85 20 93 🕐 12:30–2, 7:30–9:30. Closed Sat, Sun

Hiély-Lucullus (€€€)
Avignon's top gastronomic palace, rated as one of France's top 50 restaurants.
✉ 5 rue de la République ☎ 04 90 86 17 07 🕐 12–2, 7–10 daily

Le Petit Bedon (€€)
A lively, restaurant, popular with the local students, which serves hearty portions of Provençal cuisine and robust local wines. Good value set menu at lunchtime.
✉ 70 rue Joseph-Vernet ☎ 04 90 82 33 98 🕐 Closed Sun, Mon lunch

Simple Simon (€)
This quaint olde-worlde English tearoom serves steak and kidney pie, Bakewell tart and even Christmas pudding.
✉ 26 rue Petite-Fusterie ☎ 04 90 86 62 70 🕐 12–7. Closed Sun

Bonnieux

Le Fournil (€€)
A rustic restaurant at the heart of the Lubéron, with a charming fountain-splashed terrace for alfresco dining.
✉ 5 place Carnot ☎ 04 90 75 83 62 🕐 Closed Mon, Tue lunch

Cavaillon

Prévot (€€€)
Chef Jean-Jaques Prévot's lavish dining room is matched by equally rich cuisine. Try his *artichaut soufflé* and his succulent Cavaillon melon desserts.
✉ 353 avenue Verdun ☎ 04 90 71 32 43 🕐 Closed Sun and Mon

Châteauneuf-du-Pape

La Mère Germaine (€€)
One of the the village's most popular restaurants. The wine list includes the best *crus* of the appellation.
✉ Avenue du Commandant-Lemaître ☎ 04 90 83 54 37 🕐 Closed Tue dinner, Wed in winter

Gordes

Le Mas Tourteron (€€€)
A true taste of Provence in an 18th-century farmhouse, courtesy of Elisabeth Bourgeois' imaginative and refined regional cuisine.
✉ Chemin St-Blaise ☎ 04 90 72 00 16 🕐 Closed Mon, Tue

La Pause (€)

Tiny, friendly café-cum-teashop in the village centre serving light meals and tasty snacks.

✉ **Route Neuve** ☎ **04 90 72 11 53** 🕐 **Closed Sun eve**

Lacoste

Café de France (€)

Cheap and cheerful with *salade Niçoise* or omelette and fries for under €15.

✉ **Le Village** ☎ **04 90 75 82 25** 🕐 **Lunch only**

Lourmarin

Le Moulin de Lourmarin (€€€)

Four extravagant menus in a beautiful converted oil mill. A feast for the senses.

✉ **Rue du Temple** ☎ **04 90 68 06 69** 🕐 **Closed Tue, Wed lunch, Jan–Feb**

Ménerbes

Le Galoubet (€€)

Exquisite regional cuisine served in a small, cheerful dining room or al fresco under the olive trees.

✉ **104 avenue Marcellin Poncet** ☎ **04 90 72 36 08**

Monteux

Le Saule Pleureur (€€€)

Exceptional regional cooking from one of the Maîtres Cuisiniers of France (► panel).

✉ **145 chemin de Beauregard, Monteux (near Carpentras)** ☎ **04 90 62 01 35** 🕐 **Closed Sat lunch, Sun eve and Mon**

Orange

Le Yaka (€)

Provençal bistro with wooden beams, floral tablecloths, generous portions and a jolly atmosphere near the Théâtre Antique .

✉ **24 place Sylvian** ☎ **04 90 34 70 03** 🕐 **Closed Wed, Tue dinner in winter, Nov**

La Roselière (€)

The *saucissons* hanging from the beam overhead become appetizers in this restaurant with a small shady terrace.

✉ **4 rue du Renoyer** ☎ **04 90 34 50 42** 🕐 **Closed Tue, Wed, Nov**

Roussillon

David (€€€)

Admire the red cliffs of ochre from the terrace of this delightful restaurant. Wholesome Provençal cuisine.

✉ **Place de la Poste** ☎ **04 90 05 60 13** 🕐 **Closed Mon**

Seguret

Le Mesclun (€€)

Intimate restaurant serving regional dishes, washed down with Côtes-du-Rhône wines. Sweeping views of the Comtat Venaissin.

✉ **Rue des Poternes** ☎ **04 90 46 93 43** 🕐 **Closed Mon & Sun lunch (except Jul–Aug), Jan, Oct–Apr**

Venasque

Auberge de la Fontaine (€–€€)

This restaurant has a cosy log fire in winter and classical concerts once a month. Try the *gigot d'agneau de Venasque* and other local dishes.

✉ **Place de la Fontaine** ☎ **04 90 66 02 96** 🕐 **Closed Mon, Wed, Sun evening**

Violès

Domaine de la Tuilerie (€)

Hearty home cooking in an old farmhouse. Reservation essential.

✉ **Violès, west of Gigondas** ☎ **04 90 70 92 89** 🕐 **12–3, 8–11. Closed Tue**

Maîtres Cuisiniers

Provence and the Côte d'Azur has more than its fair share of Master Chefs (Maîtres Cuisiniers de France) – an elite association of top chefs devoted to preserving the art of French cuisine. They include Michel Philibert (Le Saule Pleureur, ► 93), Christian Etienne (Christian Etienne, ► 92), Alain Burnel (Oustau de Baumanière, ► 95), Claude Girard (Les Santons, ► 97) and Christian Willer (La Palme d'Or, ► 98).

Bouches-du-Rhône

A Prickly Plateful

Don't be surprised if you are presented with a plate of shiny, black, seaweed-draped *oursin* (sea urchins), as they are considered a great delicacy in Cassis. Simply scrape out the rosy-pink insides and eat raw with a glass of the prestigious *vin de Cassis*. Legend has it that God felt sorry for the people of Cassis and shed a tear which landed on a vine, giving birth to a dry white wine of a pale green tint, with a bouquet of heather and rosemary.

Aix-en-Provence

Autour d'une Tarte (€)

Generous slices of sweet and savoury tarts make a perfect snack. Takeaway also available.

✉ **13 rue Gaston de Saporta** ☎ **04 42 96 52 12** 🕐 **7–7. Closed Sun**

La Brocherie (€€)

Try one of the meat dishes, spit-roasted in the large chimney, or the fish at this rustic restaurant. Delicious game in season.

✉ **5 rue Fernand-Dol** ☎ **04 42 38 33 21** 🕐 **12–2, 7:30–10. Closed Sat lunch, Sun**

Café des Deux-Garçons (€€)

'Les 2 G', founded in 1792, was once the haunt of Cézanne, Picasso, Piaf and Zola. Today, with its original mirrors and chandeliers, it remains one of Aix's most elegant cafés, popular for its brasserie-style menu.

✉ **53 cours Mirabeau** ☎ **04 42 26 00 51** 🕐 **12–3, 7–11:30**

Jacquou le Croquant (€)

Tasty *tourtons* (wholewheat pancakes) with different fillings in an intimate non-smoking bistro.

✉ **2 rue de l'Aumône-Vieille** ☎ **04 42 27 37 19** 🕐 **Closed Mon, Sun in winter, Sun lunch in summer**

La Maison des Fondues (€€)

You will find 50 varieties of fondue here, from the traditional *bourguignone* to chocolate and chestnut cream dips.

✉ **13 rue de la Verrerie** ☎ **04 42 63 07 78** 🕐 **Dinner only**

Au Pain Quotidien (€)

The first Provençal outlet of a growing chain of bakery-cafés, with a country-kitchen feel. Breads, jams, condiments, ciders and coffees to buy. The open sandwiches, quiches, soups, salads and pâtisseries make an ideal lunch snack.

✉ **5 place Richelme** ☎ **04 42 23 48 57** 🕐 **8–7**

Unic Bar (€)

A perfect bar for people watching, opposite Aix's colourful fruit and vegetable market. In summer, fresh fruit juice is the speciality.

✉ **40 rue Vauvenargues** ☎ **04 42 96 38 28** 🕐 **6AM–2AM**

Yamato (€€)

An authentic,and reasonably priced Japanese restaurant.

✉ **4 rue Lieutaut** ☎ **04 42 38 00 20** 🕐 **Dinner only**

Arles

L'Affenage (€€)

Traditional fare in the converted stables of an 18th-century coaching inn.

✉ **4 rue Molière** ☎ **04 90 96 07 67** 🕐 **Closed Sun**

L'Escaladou (€)

Authentic, down-to-earth Arlésien restaurant packed with locals. Hearty helpings of *aioli*, Arles sausages and *boeuf gardian* (▶ 36–7).

✉ **23 rue Porte-de-Laure** ☎ **04 90 96 70 43** 🕐 **12–2:30, 6:30–11**

La Paillotte (€)

The decor may be simple but the menu includes fine Provençal flavours and local wines.

✉ **28 rue du Dr-Fanton** ☎ **04 90 96 33 15**

Aubagne

Le Parc (€)

Bright, sunny Provençal-style

restaurant opening onto a cool, shady park.

✉ **Avenue du 21-août-1944, Parc Jean-Moulin** ☎ **04 42 84 15 14** 🕐 **Closed Mon**

Les Baux

L'Oustau de Baumanière (€€€)

One of France's finest hotel-restaurants, visited by royalty, politicians and celebrities.

✉ **Val d'Enfer** ☎ **04 90 54 33 07** 🕐 **Closed Jan–Feb, Wed in winter**

Cassis

La Voute (€)

A heaped pan of *moules frites* washed down with *vin de Cassis* on the waterfront. Excellent value.

✉ **2 quai des Baux** ☎ **04 42 01 73 33** 🕐 **12–2:30, 7–10:30**

Eygalières

Le Bistrot d'Eygalières 'Chez Bru' (€€)

The imaginative country cooking in this small village restaurant includes pigeon served with foie gras. Delicious.

✉ **rue de la République** ☎ **04 90 90 60 34** 🕐 **Closed Mon, Tue lunch and Sun eve Oct–May**

Fontvieille

Le Patio (€€)

Traditional yet imaginative cuisine in an old farm with a pretty flower-splashed patio.

✉ **119 route du Nord** ☎ **04 90 54 73 10** 🕐 **Closed Tue dinner, Wed in winter**

Marseille

Le Mas (€)

Early birds meet night owls here for a coffee and a snack at dawn.

✉ **4 rue Lulli** ☎ **04 91 33 25 90** 🕐 **Open 24 hrs. Closed Aug**

Le Miramar (€€€)

The ultimate bouillabaisse beside the old port (▶ panel).

✉ **12 quai du Port, 13002 Marseille** ☎ **04 91 91 10 40** 🕐 **Closed Mon lunch, Sun** 🚇 **Metro (Vieux Port)**

Au Roi du Couscous (€)

The best couscous in town.

✉ **63 rue de la République** ☎ **04 91 91 45 46** 🕐 **Closed Mon** 🚌 **35, 57, 61** 🚇 **Metro (Vieux Port)**

Toinou (€–€€)

Home of Francis Rouquier, France's champion shellfish opener.

✉ **3 cours St-Louis** ☎ **04 91 33 14 94** 🕐 **12–3, 6:30–10:30** 🚌 **31, 33, 34, 41, 80, 81**

Ste-Maries-de-la-Mer

Brûleur de Loups (€€)

The tempting menu at this seafront restaurant includes *bourride* (a creamy, garlicky fish soup), fresh grilled 'catch of the day', even *carpaccio* of bull.

✉ **1 avenue Gilbert-Leroy** ☎ **04 90 97 83 31** 🕐 **12–1:45, 7–9:30. Closed Wed**

St-Rémy-de-Provence

Café des Arenes (€)

A small bar-cum-restaurant serving tasty local cuisine. Try a bull steak followed by creme brûlé with thyme. The pavement terrace enjoys the evening sun.

✉ **9 boulevard Gambetta** ☎ **04 32 60 13 43** 🕐 **Closed Tue**

Café des Arts (€)

Join the locals in St-Rémy's most popular restaurant, with its steak and frogs' legs.

✉ **30 boulevard Victor-Hugo** ☎ **04 90 92 08 50** 🕐 **Closed Mon, mid-Nov to Feb**

Bouillabaisse

This world-famous fish soup originated in Marseille as a nourishing family meal, made with choice fish kept aside by the fishermen especially for their families. It is traditionally made with up to a dozen different kinds of fish, cooked in a stock containing saffron, herbs and fennel. It is served with croutons, which are smeared with *rouille* (a sauce of fresh red chilli peppers crushed with garlic and olive oil), sprinkled with cheese then dunked in the soup.

Var & Haute-Provence

Bormes-les-Mimosas
L'Escoundudo (€€)
Enjoy wholesome regional dishes flavoured with herbs from the surrounding hills, on a sunny terrace, hidden in a steep back alley.

✉ 4 ruelle du Moulin ☎ 04 94 71 15 53 🕐 Dinner only. Closed Tue & Wed (also Sat, Sun out of season)

Lou Portaou (€€)
Hidden in a picturesque corner of Bormes, this small restaurant serves a simple menu of market-fresh Provençal cuisine. The set menus are very good value.

✉ 1 rue Cubert-des-Poètes ☎ 04 94 64 86 37 🕐 12–1:30, 7–9:30. Closed Tue

Cogolin-Marina
Le Gallon (€)
Cheap but cheerful quayside café specialising in *moules frîtes*.

✉ Quai de la Galiote, Les Marines de Cogolin ☎ 04 94 56 18 18

Collobrières
La Petite Fontaine (€)
Try some local delicacies of the Massif des Maures, washed down with wine from the local cooperative on a shady terrace. Peaceful.

✉ 1 place de la République ☎ 04 94 48 00 12 🕐 Closed Sun dinner, Mon

Digne-les-Bains
Le Grand Paris (€€)
With the reputation of Digne's best restaurant, in a former 17th-century convent. Try the pigeon accompanied by courgette flowers cooked in the juice of truffles.

✉ 19 boulevard Thiers ☎ 04 92 31 11 15 🕐 Closed Dec–Feb

Fayence
Le Castelleras (€€€)
Frogs legs wrapped in pastry with cream and chives is one of many local specialities served in this old stone *mas*.

✉ Route de Seillans ☎ 04 94 76 13 80 🕐 Closed Mon, Tue

Forcalquier
Hostellerie des Deux Lions (€€€)
This smart hotel restaurant is celebrated for its delicious game fish dishes. Booking essential.

✉ 11 place du Bourget ☎ 04 92 75 25 30 🕐 Closed Tue, Wed

Gap
Le Tourton des Alpes (€€)
The local speciality of *tourtons* – tiny hot pastry envelopes filled with either potato, spinach, meat, prune or apple – are served here in copious quantities.

✉ 1 rue des Cordiers ☎ 04 92 53 90 91 🕐 Daily

La Garde-Freinet
Auberge Sarrasine (€€)
This cosy, intimate restaurant at the heart of the Massif des Maures provides the perfect venue to taste *cassoulet Provençal* (hotpot of white beans, pork and white wine) by the log fire in winter.

✉ D558, Massif des Maures ☎ 04 94 55 59 60 🕐 Closed Sun eve & Mon

Grimaud
Les Santons (€€)
Classic cuisine and impeccable service in elegant Provençal surroundings. Les Santons is most definitely one of the region's top restaurants.

✉ Route Nationale ☎ 04 94 43 21 02 🕐 Closed Tue, Wed, Thu lunch, Nov–Mar

Les Issambres
Villa Saint-Elme (€€€)
One of the coast's most spectacular restaurant terraces, with exceptional cuisine to match. Try the lobster tart followed by *pigeon en croûte*.

✉ **Corniche des Issambres** ☎ 04 94 49 52 52 🕐 12–3:45, 7:30–9:45

Miramar
La Marine (€€)
Possibly the best sardines on the Corniche d'Or, on a breezy terrace overhanging the Mediterranean.

✉ **Port de Miramar** ☎ 04 93 75 49 30 🕐 **Closed out of season**

Moustiers-Ste-Marie
La Bastide de Moustiers (€€)
Dine in the country home of the world's top chef, Alain Ducasse. Despite the reputation it remains surprisingly affordable (▶ panel).

✉ **Chemin de Quinson, 04360 la Grisolière** ☎ 04 92 70 47 47

Les Santons (€€)
Widespread reputation for good food and a pretty setting.

✉ **Place de l'Église** ☎ 04 92 74 66 48 🕐 **Closed Tue, Jan, mid-Nov to mid-Dec**

Sisteron
Hôtel Restaurant de la Citadelle (€€)
Enjoy a spectacular alpine panorama whilst trying local delicacies *fougasse à l'anchois* (anchovy stuffed bread) or Sisteron lamb with thyme and rosemary.

✉ **126 rue Saunerie** ☎ 04 92 61 13 52 🕐 **Closed Nov, Feb**

St-Tropez
La Bouillabaisse (€€)
A speciality fish restaurant in a traditional fisherman's cottage on the beach.

✉ **Plage de la Bouillabaisse** ☎ 04 94 97 54 00 🕐 **Closed mid-Oct to mid-Feb**

Cafés des Arts (€€)
A favourite haunt of the see-and-be-seen brigade since the 1960s. You come for the fun, not the food.

✉ **Place des Lices** ☎ 04 94 97 02 25 🕐 8AM–midnight

La Citadelle (€€)
This tiny atmospheric restaurant spills out on to the street. Don't miss the tarte tatin.

✉ **1 rue Aire du Cjemin** ☎ 04 94 54 81 19 🕐 Apr–Sep 12–2, 7–10:30

L'Eau a la Bouche (€–€€)
Simple, homely cuisine on a sunny pavement terrace in a cobbled backstreet near the Chapelle de la Misericorde. Excellent value.

✉ **43 rue du Portail Neuf** ☎ 06 19 73 42 53

La Table du Marché (€–€€)
This smart bistro-cum-deli offers an array of light snacks, regional specialities, patisseries and wines. It also serves afternoon tea.

✉ **38 rue Georges Clemenceau** ☎ 04 94 97 85 20 🕐 **Closed Mon eve, Wed and winter.**

Vien Dong (€€)
The exotic Vietnamese, Chinese and Thai dishes make a pleasant change from Provençal cuisine, but the main attraction is that the restaurant is owned by a former Mr Universe.

✉ **avenue Paul-Roussel** ☎ 04 94 97 09 78

Alain Ducasse
Don't expect to find Monsieur Ducasse himself in the kitchen at La Bastide de Moustiers as he is far too busy looking after his restaurant in Paris, having left the famous Louis XV in Monaco (▶ 98). Instead he has entrusted the cooking to star pupil, Monegasque Sonia Lee, who delights her guests with sensational dishes that embrace all the flavours and perfumes of Haute-Provence.

Alpes-Maritimes

Nice's Top Chef
Irresistable local dishes such as *pate au pistou* and *tripes Niçoise* are the trademarks of Dominic Le Stanc, former chef of the Negresco's famous Chantecler restaurant, and a name synonymous with the very best in Provençal cuisine. He now owns La Mérenda – a tiny rustic restaurant which he runs with his wife – a temple of Niçois cuisine.

Antibes

Le Bacon (€€€)
One of the coast's best fish restaurants, with exceptional views over old Antibes.
✉ Boulevard Bacon, Cap-d'Antibes ☎ 04 93 61 50 02 ⏰ Closed Mon, and Tue lunch (except Jul–Aug), Nov–Jan

Biot

Auberge du Jarrier (€€)
Imaginative cuisine and an unmistakable Provençal flavour in an old jar factory.
✉ 30 passage de la Bourgade ☎ 04 93 65 11 68 ⏰ Closed Mon, and Tue lunch

Cannes

La Palme d'Or (€€€)
Join the stars at Cannes' most prestigious restaurant, to experience some of prize-winning master chef Christian Willer's latest culinary creations.
✉ Hotel Martinez ☎ 04 92 98 74 14 ⏰ Closed Sun & Mon

Èze

La Bergerie (€€)
Traditional dishes with a good choice of Côtes-de-Provence wines. Winter by the open fire, summer on the shady terrace overlooking the sea.
✉ Grande Corniche Èze ☎ 04 93 41 03 67 ⏰ Dinner only. Sun only in winter

La Chèvre d'Or (€€€)
Breathtaking sea views and inspired French cuisine.
✉ 3 rue du Barri ☎ 04 92 10 66 66 ⏰ Closed mid-Nov to Feb

Haut-de-Cagnes

Le Sant Elena (€)
A small café-restaurant beside the castle, specialising in local dishes such as *mesclun* and *petits farcis*.
✉ 1 place Grimaldi ☎ 06 13 86 71 48

Juan-les-Pins

L'Oasis (€€)
Dine on the beach at this restaurant, with views sweeping from the Cap-d'Antibes to the Îles Lérins.
✉ Boulevard Littoral ☎ 04 93 61 45 15 ⏰ Dinner only

Menton

Don Cicco (€)
Italian cuisine a kilometre from the Italian border.
✉ 11 rue St-Michel ☎ 04 93 57 92 92 ⏰ Closed Wed

La Mediterranée (€)
Highly recommended for fish lovers.
✉ 27 quai de Monléon ☎ 04 93 90 03 47

Monaco

Louis XV (€€€)
Should you break the bank at the Casino, come to the Louis XV, with its three Michelin rosettes.
✉ Hotel de Paris, place du Casino ☎ 0377 92 16 29 76 ⏰ Closed Tue, Wed

Zebra Square (€€)
Rub shoulders with the beautiful people on the sun terrace of this chic Mediterranean restaurant where even the crockery has zebra stripes.
✉ 10 avenue Princesse-Grace, Monte-Carlo ☎ 0377 99 99 25 50

Mougins

Le Moulin de Mougins (€€€)
A bastion of Provençal cuisine, headed by celebrated chef Alain Llorca (formerly of Chantecler, the

top Niçois restaurant) since spring 2004.

✉ Notre-Dame de Vie ☎ 04 93 75 78 24 🕔 Closed Mon

Les Muscadins (€€€)

A poor, young artist called Picasso stayed here once. To pay for his accommodation he painted murals on his bedroom walls, but the outraged owner made him whitewash over them. The restaurant now serves delicious regional cuisine with Italian influences.

✉ 18 boulevard Courteline ☎ 04 92 28 28 28 🕔 Closed Tue & Thu

Nice

Aphridite (€€)

The imaginative culinary creations of chef David Faure are a seductive blend of classic French and Nissart cuisine.

✉ 10 boulevard Dubancharge ☎ 04 93 85 63 53 🕔 Closed Sun, Mon 🚌 38

Chantecler (€€€)

Nice's leading restaurant and a bastion of French gastronomy.

✉ Hôtel Negresco, 37 promenade des Anglais ☎ 04 93 16 64 00 🕔 15 Nov–15 Dec 🚌 3, 8, 9, 10, 11, 12, 23, 34

Fenocchio (€)

The best ice creams on the Côte d'Azur.

✉ Place Rossetti ☎ 04 93 80 72 52 🕔 9AM–midnight 🚌 All buses

Flo (€€)

Brasserie in a converted art-deco theatre with the kitchen on stage! Special late night menu up to midnight.

✉ 4 rue Sacha-Guitry ☎ 04 93 13 38 38 🕔 12–3, 7–midnight 🚌 1, 2, 4, 5, 9, 10, 14, 22, 23, 24

Lou Pilha Leva (€)

Niçois fast-food (► panel).

✉ 10 rue du Collet ☎ 04 93 13 99 08 🕔 8–11 (midnight in summer) 🚌 All buses

La Mérenda (€€)

Irresistible menu of Nissart specialities, prepared by one of France's outstanding chefs (► panel 98).

✉ 4 rue de la Terrace 🕔 Closed Sat–Sun, hols 🚌 All buses ❓ Credit cards not accepted

La Petite Maison (€€)

Local market-fresh dishes near the Opèra. The hors-d'oeuvres Niçois is a meal in itself. Book well in advance.

✉ 11 rue St-François-de-Paule ☎ 04 93 92 59 59 🕔 Closed Sun 🚌 All buses

La Rotonde (€)

The Riviera's most original brasserie. Bright merry-go-round décor complete with flashing lights, automats and painted wooden horses.

✉ Hôtel Negresco, 37 promenade des Anglais ☎ 04 93 16 64 00 🕔 7AM–11PM 🚌 3, 8, 9, 10, 11, 12, 23, 34

Le Transsiberien (€€)

An epic culinary journey of bortsch and blinis in a great Trans-Siberian rail carriage.

✉ 1 rue Bottero ☎ 04 93 96 49 05 🕔 Closed Sun, Mon 🚌 6, 7, 9, 10, 12, 23

St-Paul-de-Vence

Mas d'Artigny (€€€)

Well known for its fruits de mer and fish dishes. Not cheap but worth every euro.

✉ Route de la Colle ☎ 04 93 32 84 54

Lou Pilha Leva

'Lou Pilha Leva' in local Nissart patois means 'you take away'. At the heart of old Nice, this hole-in-the-wall serves piping hot plates of socca, pissaladière, beignets, farcis, pizza and other Niçois specialities (► 36–37) – €7 will buy you a bit of everything! Ideal for a snack lunch, the trestle tables provide the perfect opportunity to chat to the locals.

Vaucluse

Prices
Expect to pay the following per night:

€ = up to €50
€€ = up to €100
€€€ = over €100

Île de la Barthelasse
This island on the Rhône has had a colourful and varied history. Once a hunting reserve, it then became a gathering place of Avignonais prostitutes and thieves, but in later years it was a fashionable place to promenade and picnic. Today it is still a popular recreation site with a lovely open-air swimming pool, campsites and several *chambres d'hôtes*.

Hotel websites
www.auberge-luberon-peuzin.com
www.hotelprestige-provence.com
www.hotel-laferme.com
www.mirande.fr
www.labeaume.com
www.bournereau.com
www.le-beffroi.com

Apt
Auberge du Lubéron (€€)
Apt's top hotel, beside the river.
✉ 8 place du Faubourg du Ballet ☎ 04 90 74 12 50 ⏰ Closed mid-Nov to mid-Jan

Avignon
Auberge de Cassagne (€€€)
Ancient Provençal dwelling five minutes from Avignon, with beautiful gardens, outdoor pool and a gastonomic restaurant of international renown.
✉ 450 allée de Cassagne, le Pontet ☎ 04 90 31 04 18

La Ferme (€)
Old farmhouse on the Île de la Barthelasse (► panel). Gypsy caravans in the garden are popular with actors during the summer festival.
✉ Chemin des Bois, Île de la Barthelasse ☎ 04 90 82 57 53 ⏰ Closed Nov to mid-Mar

La Mirande (€€€)
Elegant hotel in a medieval cardinal's palace, on a quiet cobbled square at the foot of the Popes' Palace.
✉ 4 place de la Mirande ☎ 04 90 85 93 93

Bonnieux
De l'Aiguebrun (€€)
A beautiful old, stone farmhouse 6km east of Bonnieux, peacefully located at the heart of the Lubéron National Park.
✉ Relais de la Canube ☎ 04 90 04 47 00

Gordes
Le Mas de la Beaume (€€)
A beautiful stone mas overlooking the village, with five rooms – each traditionally-furnished with consummate taste –a picturesque garden, swimming pool and a Jacuzzi. There is even a fantastic farmhouse-style breakfast.
✉ 84220 Gordes Village ☎ 04 90 72 02 96, fax: 04 90 72 06 89

Lourmarin
Hostellerie le Paradou (€€)
Small, sleepy hotel beneath the gorges of Lourmarin.
✉ Combe de Lourmarin (D943) ☎ 04 90 68 04 05

Monteux
Domaine de Bournereau (€€)
This 250-year-old restored farm property is a veritable oasis of Provençal calm, with spectacular views of Mont Ventoux, 12 spacious, elegant rooms, extensive gardens and outdoor pool.
✉ 579 Chemin de la Sorguette ☎ 04 90 66 36 13, fax: 04 90 66 36 93

Orange
Arène (€€)
Small three-star hotel in a quiet traffic-free square in the historic town centre.
✉ 8 place de Langes ☎ 04 90 11 40 40 ⏰ Closed mid to late Nov

Roussillon
Mamaison (€€)
Small old farmhouse with rooms decorated by local artists and a restaurant which specialises in home-grown organic vegetarian dishes.
✉ Quartier Les Devens ☎ 04 90 05 74 17

Vaison-la-Romaine
Hostellerie le Beffroi (€€)
Atmospheric hotel in Vaison's ancient *haute ville*.
✉ 2 place Monfort ☎ 04 90 36 04 71 ⏰ Closed Jan–Feb

Bouches-du-Rhône

Aix

Des Augustins (€€€)
Intriguing blend of history and modernity within a 15th-century former Augustinian convent.
✉ 3 rue de la Masse ☎ 04 42 27 28 59 🕓 Closed mid-Jan to mid-Feb

Le Pigonnet (€€€)
Beautiful family-run *bastide* hotel with antique furniture, rose arbours and views over the countryside.
✉ 5 avenue du Pigonnet ☎ 04 42 59 02 90

Arles

Arlatan
This charming 16th-century residence of the comtes d'Arlatan is one of the region's most beautiful historic hotels, with 30 rooms individually decorated with Provençal antiques.
✉ 26 rue Sauvage ☎ 04 90 93 56 66

Le Calendal (€€)
Stylish Provençal mansion. Some rooms overlook the Roman arena.
✉ 5 rue Porte de Laure ☎ 04 90 96 11 89

Nord-Pinus (€€€)
Unique hotel and a classified national monument. This is a hotel of strong literary connections, once a favourite haunt of the Félibres poets, and other literati, including Stendhal, Mistral, Cocteau and Henry James. Today it is popular with Christian Lacroix, top matadors and other wealthy aficionados, and is decorated accordingly with bullfighting posters and trophies. Without doubt the place for people who want to feel truly Arlésien!
✉ Place du Forum ☎ 04 90 93 44 44 🕓 Closed Jan–Mar

Fontvieille

Auberge de la Régalido (€€€)
Warm, friendly *auberge* in a converted oil mill.
✉ Rue Frédéric-Mistral ☎ 04 90 54 60 22 🕓 Closed Jan

Marseille

Le Corbusier (€)
Part of an avant-garde experiment in architectural design by Le Corbusier (► panel).
✉ 280 boulevard Michelet, 8e. ☎ 04 91 16 78 00 🔲 21, 21S, 22, 22S

Mercure Beauvau Vieux-Port (€€€)
Overlooking the port and often used as a backdrop in films. Past guests include Chopin, George Sand, Cocteau and Hemingway.
✉ 4 rue Beauvau ☎ 04 91 54 91 00 🚇 Metro (Vieux Port)

St-Pierre-les-Aubagne

Hostellerie de la Source (€€)
Small three-star hotel near Aubagne. Garden, pool and tennis court.
☎ 04 42 04 09 19

St-Rémy-de-Provence

Hotel Les Ateliers de L'Image (€€€)
An oasis of sophisticated minimalism at the heart of the town with a tranquil garden, outdoor pool and an exotic Franco-Japanese restaurant.
✉ 36 Boulevard Victor Hugo ☎ 04 90 92 51 50

Stes-Maries-de-la-Mer

Hotel de Cacharel (€€)
A former *gardian* ranch in the heart of the marshes. Horse riding and bull watching.
✉ Route de Cacharel ☎ 04 90 97 95 44 🕓 Closed Nov–Mar

La Cité Radieuse
In 1952 Le Corbusier built a massive 17-storey concrete building intended to be part of a 6-block Cité Radieuse (Radiant City), designed as a prototype for 'vertical living', combining living space, shops, schools and recreational facilities all under one roof. Sadly it looks far from radiant and Marseillais soon dubbed it the 'madman's house'.

Hotel websites
www.hotelpigonnet.com
www.hotel-arlatan.fr
www.nord-pinus.com
www.bestofprovence.com
www.mercure.com
www.lcm.fr/lasource.htm
www.hotelphoto.com
www.hotel-cacharel.com

Var & Haute-Provence

A Hotel for All Seasons
The exclusive new Four Seasons Resort Provence at Terre Blanche (£££) near Tourettes comprises a series of modern deluxe villas gathered around a hilltop bar and restaurant area and leading down to two world-class golf courses and a clubhouse restaurant. There are also health and fitness suites, and superb business facilities – even broadband links beside each sunlounger at the swimming pool. Built on land formerly belonging to Sean Connery, the entire complex has been designed to resemble a Provençal village and offers a real getaway from the hustle and bustle of the Riviera.
www.fourseasons.com/provence
☎ 04 94 39 90 00

Hotel websites
www.lamaisondumonde.com
www.aubergeduchoucas.com
www.villamarie.fr

Bormes les Mimosas
Le Bellevue (€)
A simple Logis de France establishment with spectacular views to the sea.
✉ 12 place Gambetta ☎ 04 94 71 15 15 🕐 Closed Oct–Jan

Cogolin
La Maison du Monde (€€)
This small, homely hotel with just 12 rooms, a shady garden and an outdoor pool at the bustling heart of Cogolin, offers affordable accommodation for those wishing to worship the Tropezienne sun without paying St-Tropez prices.
✉ 63 rue Carnot, Cogolin ☎ 04 94 54 77 54, fax: 04 94 54 77 55

Forcalquier
Hostellerie des Deux-Lions (€€)
Charming old coaching inn with rustic decor and delicious local dishes.
✉ 11 place du Bourguet ☎ 04 92 75 25 30 🕐 Closed Jan–Feb

Grand Cañon du Verdon
Hôtel-Restaurant du Grand Canyon (€€€)
Rooms with great views.
✉ Falaise des Cavaliers, D71, Aiguines ☎ 04 94 76 91 31

Gréoux-les-Bains
Villa Borghese (€€)
A delightful hotel with flower-filled balconies, charming garden and pool.
www.villa-borghese.com
✉ Avenue des Thermes ☎ 04 92 78 00 91 🕐 Closed mid-Nov to mid-Mar

Monêtier-les-Bains
L'Auberge du Choucas (€€)
Cosy farmhouse high in the Alps, and ideal for skiing at Serre Chevalier.
✉ Monêtier-les-Bains, 14km N of Briançon ☎ 04 92 24 42 73 🕐 Closed Nov to mid-Dec

Moustiers-Ste-Marie
La Bonne Auberge (€)
Clean, modest hotel near the great Verdon gorges. Popular with walkers.
✉ Route de Castellane ☎ 04 92 74 66 18 🕐 Closed Dec–Jan

St-Tropez
Château de la Messardiere (€€€)
St-Tropez' most luxurious hotel. Truly palatial.
✉ Route de Tahiti ☎ 04 94 56 76 00 🕐 Closed Dec–Feb

Mas de Chastelas (€€€)
Stay with Depardieu, Belmondo and other French film idols at this beautiful 18th-century *mas*, just outside St-Tropez.
✉ Quartier Bertaud, Gassin ☎ 04 94 56 71 71 🕐 Closed Nov & Dec

Villa Marie (€€€)
On the hill overlooking Pampelonne, this chic boutique hotel and spa, stylishly decorated with terracotta, wrought iron and St Tropez azure, is *the* new address for the beautiful people.
✉ Ramatuelle, near St-Tropez ☎ 04 94 97 40 22, fax: 04 94 97 37 55

St-Véran
Les Chalets du Villard (€€)
Traditional alpine chalet accommodation in the highest village in Europe.
✉ St-Véran ☎ 04 92 45 82 08 🕐 Closed mid-Sep to mid-Dec, mid-Apr to mid-Jun

Alpes-Maritimes

Cannes
Martinez (€€€)
This deluxe hotel contains Cannes' top restaurant, La Palme d'Or – excellent for star spotting during the Film Festival

🖂 73 boulevard de la Croisette ☎ 04 92 98 73 00

Cap-d'Antibes
Hôtel du Cap-Eden-Roc (€€€)
'A large, proud, rose-coloured hotel. Deferential palms cool its flushed façade, and before it stretches a ... bright tan prayer rug of a beach.'
(F Scott Fitzgerald *Tender is the Night*)

🖂 Boulevard Kennedy ☎ 04 93 61 39 01 🕐 Open mid-Apr to mid-Oct

Èze
Château Eza (€€€)
A collection of medieval houses, linked together to form a luxury eagle's nest.

🖂 Rue de la Pise ☎ 04 93 41 12 24

Monaco
Hôtel de Paris (€€€)
Monte-Carlo's most prestigious address.

🖂 Place du Casino ☎ 0377 92 16 30 00

Nice
Château des Ollières (€€€)
Exclusive *belle-époque* villa, once owned by a Russian prince.

🖂 39 avenue des Baumettes ☎ 04 92 15 77 99 🚌 6, 9, 10, 12, 23, 26

Hôtel Hi (€€)
Quirky new hotel with wacky modern furnishings, an organic 24-hour canteen, a hammam and a beach on the roof.

🖂 3 avenue des Fleurs ☎ 04 97 07 26 26

Negresco (€€€)
World-famous hotel in the *belle-époque* style with a renowned restaurant (► 99)

🖂 37 promenade des Anglais ☎ 04 93 16 64 00 🚌 6, 7, 9, 10, 12, airport bus

Palais Maeterlinck (€€€)
Once the home of poet Maurice Maeterlinck, now a palatial, modern coastal hotel.

🖂 30 boulevard Maurice-Maeterlinck ☎ 04 92 00 72 00 🚌 14

Palais de la Méditerranée (€€€)
This luxury seafront hotel has 188 lavish rooms and suites with all mod cons, a heated outdoor pool and spa, and a panoramic terrace.

🖂 Promenade des Anglais ☎ 04 92 14 77 00

Solara (€)
Excellent value in Nice's chic pedestrian zone.

🖂 7 rue de France ☎ 04 93 88 09 96

St-Jean-Cap-Ferrat
Grand Hotel du Cap-Ferrat (€€€)
Sumptuous palace, in lush, tropical gardens, amid some of the world's most expensive real estate.

🖂 Boulevard Géneral-de-Gaulle ☎ 04 93 76 50 50

St-Paul-de-Vence
La Colomb d'Or (€€€)
Once a modest 1920s café where Braque, Matisse, Picasso and Léger paid for their drinks with canvases. Now a deluxe hotel.

🖂 Place du Général-de-Gaulle ☎ 04 93 32 80 02

Famous Guests
Charlie Chaplin taught his children to swim in the pool of the Grand Hôtel du Cap-Ferrat. Queen Victoria was one of the first famous residents of the Hôtel de Paris; Michael Jackson one of the more recent.

Hotel websites
www.hotel-martinez.com
www.edenroc-hotel.fr
www.shl.com/eza
www.montecarloresort.com
www.chateaudesollieres.com
www.hi-hotel.net
www.hotel-negresco-nice.com
www.lepalaisdelamediterranee.com
www.palais-maeterlinck.com
www.grand-hotel-cap-ferrat.com
www.la-colombe-dor.com

Provençal Souvenirs & Gifts

Opening Hours
Most shops in Provence and the Côte d'Azur are open from Tuesday to Saturday between 8 or 10–12 and 2–6, although some stay open longer at the height of the summer season or during festival times.

A Ray of Sunshine
Souleiado is a Provençal word meaning 'a sun-ray piercing through the clouds' and is the name of the leading manufacturer of block-printed Provençal textiles. The company was founded in 1938 by Charles Demery in a successful attempt to revive a 200 year-old textile industry in Tarascon. The Musée Souleiado (✉ 39 rue Proudhon, Tarascon ☎ 04 90 91 08 80 ⊙ By appointment only) includes 40,000 18th-century fruitwood blocks which are still the basis for all the Souleiado patterns today.

Vaucluse

Roussillon
Cannelle
Small shop jam-packed with fun gift ideas, regional produce (olive oils, liqueurs, saffron), books and perfumes.
✉ **Place de la Poste** ☎ 04 90 05 71 27

Bouches-du-Rhône

Arles
L'Arlésienne
Traditional Camarguais costumes.
✉ **12 rue du Président-Wilson** ☎ 04 90 93 28 05

Bijouterie Pinus
Necklaces, bracelets and crosses in traditional Provençal designs.
✉ **6 rue Jean-Jaurès** ☎ 04 90 96 04 63

Aubagne
L'Atelier d'Art
Manufacturer of faience and *santons* (small terracotta figures dressed or painted in regional costumes) in Aubagne, the pottery capital of France.
✉ **2 boulevard Émile-Combes** ☎ 04 42 70 12 92

Marseille
La Compagnie de Provence
One of Marseille's few remaining specialist soap shops.
✉ **1 rue Caisserie, 13002 Marseille** ☎ 04 91 56 20 94
🚇 **Metro (Vieux Port)**

St-Rémy-de-Provence
Les Olivades
Colour-drenched printed fabrics, traditional Provençal clothing and gift ideas can be found here.
✉ **28 rue Lafayette** ☎ 04 90 92 00 80

Var and Haute-Provence

Digne-les-Bains
La Maison de la Lavande
Every imaginable lavender product is available here – they even sell a lavender liqueur.
✉ **38 boulevard Gassendi** ☎ 04 92 31 33 94

St-Tropez
Pierre Basset
Terracotta and enamelled tiles, jars, pots and vases in sunny colours.
✉ **Route des Plages** ☎ 04 94 97 75 06

Alpes-Maritimes

Biot
Verrerie de Biot
Traditional bubble-flecked glassware from Provence's capital of glass-blowing makes an unusual souvenir or gift.
✉ **Chemin des Combes** ☎ 04 93 65 03 00 .

Grasse
Parfumerie Fragonard
The very finest perfumes from Provence. They also offer visitors interesting guided tours (► 88).
✉ **20 boulevard Fragonard** ☎ 04 93 36 44 65

Nice
Parfums Poilpot
Tiny, traditional perfumerie with a wide choice of scents from Grasse.
✉ **10 rue St-Gaëtan** ☎ 04 93 85 60 77
🚌 **All buses**

Fashion

Vaucluse

Avignon
Alain Manoukian
Chic, affordable women's clothing by a local designer available here.
✉ 23 rue des Marchands
☎ 04 90 27 96 02

La Boutique du Sac
Buy an extra bag for all your souvenirs.
✉ 15 rue Josef Vernet ☎ 04 90 85 61 39

Mouret Chapelier
One of France's few traditional milliners.
✉ 20 rue des Marchands
☎ 04 90 85 39 38

Roussillon
Garance
Chunky multi-coloured costume jewellery and fun fabric handbags.
✉ Place de la Mairie ☎ 04 90 05 81 57

Bouches-du-Rhône

Aix
Petit Boy
Children's fashions from 6 months to 16 years.
✉ 6 rue Aude ☎ 04 42 93 13 05

Arles
Christian Lacroix
The boutique of the world-famous Arles-born designer (► panel).
✉ 52 rue de la République
☎ 04 90 96 11 16

Gallia Style
Smart shoes for sale in a restored 12th-century monastery.
✉ 36 rue de la République
☎ 04 90 96 10 36

Var and Haute-Provence

Gap
Blanc-Gras Sport
The latest fashions in ski clothing and equipment.
✉ 39 rue St-Arey ☎ 04 92 53 95 21

St-Tropez
Blanc Bleu
Stylish, sporty fashion for both sexes.
✉ 3 rue Allard ☎ 04 94 97 04 29

Hermès
The ultimate in French chic.
✉ place Grammond ☎ 04 94 97 04 29

Alpes-Maritimes

Biot
Chacok
Bright colours and bold designs by Biot designer Arlette Chacok in Biot.
✉ Route de la Mer, Biot
☎ 04 93 65 60 60

Monaco
Cravatterie Nazionali
Designer ties.
✉ 17 avenue Spélinques ☎ 0377/93 50 88 80

Society Club
Men will love this stylish, macho shop selling the latest in designer labels such as D&G, Boss and YSL.
✉ Centre Commercial le Métropole ☎ 0377 93 25 25 01

St-Paul-de-Vence
Bleu Comme là-Bas
A wacky, bright orange jewellery shop owned by a young, imaginative designer. Affordable and fun.
✉ 38 rue Grande
☎ 04 93 32 04 17

Local Genius
Christian Lacroix was born in Arles under the star sign of Taurus, the symbol of Camargue. One of haute-couture's most innovative and eclectic designers, his clothes are classic yet daring, feminine yet boldly Mediterranean, frequently inspired by the traditional Arlésian costumes. The fashions, jewellery, hats and handbags of his flamboyant boutique at the very heart of Arles' pedestrian zone represent a fashion mecca for the rich and fashionable.

Food & Drink

Too Many Sweets Give You Tooth Aix!

The traditional souvenirs of Aix are its *calissons*, delicious almond and melon sweets first created in 1473 and still made in the traditional way by mixing ground almonds with glazed melons and fruit syrup. Beautifully packaged and best bought from Béchard or Riederer (✉ 6 rue Thiers), they make excellent presents (if you can resist eating them all yourself).

Vaucluse

Apt
Aptunion
Apt claims to be the world leader in crystallised fruits and this is the top shop in town. Phone in advance for a factory tour.
✉ N100 (direction Avignon) ☎ 04 90 76 31 43

Avignon
Les Halles
This modern, covered farmers market is the perfect place to buy for a picnic.
✉ Place Pie 🕐 Tue–Sun 6AM–1PM

Gordes
Oliviers & Co
Small but beautiful shop specialising in Provençal olives and their derivative products including olive chutney, *tapenades*, oils and pastas.
✉ rue de la Poste ☎ No telephone

L'Isle-sur-la-Sorgue
Les Délices du Lubéron
A tasty selection of olive oil, *tapenades*, herbs, nougats, candies and other regional products.
✉ Avenue du Partage-des-Eaux ☎ 04 90 20 77 37

Roussillon
Au Goût du Jour
An upmarket deli combining regional honeys, oils, wines and cheeses with tea and champagne.
✉ 5 rue Richard Casteau ☎ 04 32 52 17 68

Vaison-la-Romaine
Lou Canesteou
Considered Vaison's best cheese shop, offering a wide choice of locally made *chèvre* including *banon* (wrapped in oak leaves), *picadon* and *cachat*.
✉ 10 rue Raspail ☎ 04 90 36 31 30

Bouches-du-Rhône

Mouriès
Moulin à Huile Coopératif du Mas Neuf
This unlikely looking shed sells some of the best olive oil in France.
✉ Off D17 (direction Eyguières) ☎ 04 90 47 53 86 🕐 Mon–Sat 9–12, 2–6; Sun 10–12, 2–6

Aix
Chocolaterie Puyricard
Puyricard's handmade chocolates are considered the finest in France. Visit their traditional chocolate factory in a northern suburb.
✉ Quartier Beaufort, Puyricard ☎ 04 42 96 11 21

Maison Béchard
An old-fashioned sweetshop, well known for its *calissons*.
✉ 12 cours Mirabeau ☎ 04 42 26 06 78

Aubagne
Distillerie Janot
Tastings of *pastis*, Provence's most popular liqueur. Visits by appointment only.
✉ Avenue du Pastre, ZI les Paluds ☎ 04 42 82 29 57

Marseille
Le Four des Navettes
This is Marseille's oldest bakery. Try the famous orange-flower *navette* biscuits, in the shape of the Stes Maries' legendary boat (► 57), originally only made for the Catholic feast day of

Candlemas.

📧 136 rue Sainte ☎ 04 91 33 32 12 🚌 55, 61, 81

Torrefaction Noailles
Mouth-watering sweetshop-cum-tea salon.

📧 56 La Canebière ☎ 04 91 55 60 66 🚇 Métro 2 (Noailles)

St-Rémy-de-Provence
La Cave aux Fromages
Cheeses from throughout France, including regional specialities.

📧 1 place Hilaire ☎ 04 90 92 32 45

Le Petit Duc
This old-fashioned sweet shop prides itself on its traditional recipes, made entirely without artificial additives or preservatives.

📧 7 boulevard Victor Hugo ☎ 04 90 92 08 31

Var and Haute-Provence

Gap
Les 4 Saisons
Delicious mountain produce – fruit, vegetables, cheeses, truffles, pâtés, honey and herbs.

📧 Place aux Herbes ☎ 04 92 53 63 42

St-Tropez (Gassin)
Petit Village
Stocks the wines of the Maîtres Vignerons of St-Tropez.

📧 Carrefour de la Foux, Gassin ☎ 04 94 56 32 04

Alpes-Maritimes

Cannes
Ceneri
One of France's top cheese stores with over 300

different types, from huge rounds of runny brie to tiny *boutons de culotte* (trouser-button) goat's cheese.

📧 22 rue Meynadier ☎ 04 93 39 63 68

Nice
Alziari
This old family shop presses their own olive oil and sells *olives de Nice* by the kilo. A veritable Niçois institution.

📧 14 rue Saint-François-de-Paule ☎ 04 93 85 76 92 🚌 All buses

Caprioglio
Wine store in old Nice, to suit all purses from *vin de table* (stored in giant orange tanks) to the top *crus*.

📧 16 rue de la Préfecture ☎ 04 93 85 66 57 🚌 All buses

Espuno
One of France's best bakeries. Try the regional *fougasse*.

📧 35 rue Droite ☎ 04 93 80 50 67 🚌 All buses

Maison Auer
Nice's last traditional maker of crystallised fruits, famed throughout France.

📧 7 rue St-François-de-Paule ☎ 04 93 85 77 98 🚌 All buses

St-Paul-de-Vence
La Petite Cave de Saint-Paul
An authentic 14th-century cellar containing a choice selection of Provençal wines, including those produced in the surrounding vineyards.

📧 7 rue de l'Etoile ☎ 04 93 32 59 54

The Art of Drinking Pastis
Ice cubes first, then pastis, then water – a hallowed trio for a great Provençal custom – the *apéritif*. There are many different ways to drink pastis – *noyé* (drowned) with lots of water, *en flanc*, thick and strong, with very little water or as a cocktail. Try the 'parrot' (with mint syrup), the 'tomato' (with grenadine) or the 'Moorish' (with a bitter almond syrup). *Santé!*

Art, Antiquities & Books

Books for Tea

Avignon booksellers certainly know how best to sell their books, accompanied by a good cup of tea and a *pâtisserie*! There's nothing more enjoyable than browsing through your newly purchased book over scones and cream on the sun-drenched patio of Shakespeare in Avignon.

Vaucluse

Avignon

Hervé Baum

Modern and antique, chic and rustic – objects for home and garden.

✉ **19 rue Petite Fusterie** ☎ **04 90 86 37 66**

Shakespeare

A discount English bookshop and tea shop. Occasional readings and recitals too. (► panel).

✉ **155 rue Carreterie** ☎ **04 90 27 38 50**

L'Isle-sur-la-Sorgue

L'Isle aux Brocantes

There are over 35 dealers here, with a wide variety of items, trading in an 'antique village' emporium.

✉ **Passage du Pont, 7 avenue des 4-Otages** ☎ **04 90 20 69 93**

Roussillon

Galerie des Ocres

Gifts and paints in every imaginable shade of ochre from France's Grand Cañon (► 24–5).

✉ **Le Castrum** ☎ **04 90 05 62 99**

Bouches-du-Rhône

Aix

Librairie de Provence

Large bookshop with an excellent choice of regional travel, literature and culinary titles.

✉ **31 cours Mirabeau** ☎ **04 42 26 07 23**

Yves Ungaro

An aladdin's cave of pictures and objets d'art at the heart of Aix's antiques quarter.

✉ **1 rue Jaubert** ☎ **04 42 63 22 94**

Arles

Antiquités Maurin

A treasure trove of regional furniture, paintings and ceramics from the 17th to the 20th century. Worldwide shipping service available.

✉ **4 rue de Grille** ☎ **04 90 96 51 57**

Librairie Actes Sud

The bookshop of Arles' Actes Sud publishing house, in Le Méjan, a lively arts complex with a bar, cinema, restaurant and record shop.

✉ **43 rue du Docteur-Fanton** ☎ **04 90 49 56 77** 🕒 **Daily 10–9 except Mon (2–9), Thu (10–7)**

Les Baux

Le Mas des Chevaliers

Traditional Provençal furniture and objets d'art.

✉ **Vallon de la Fontaine** ☎ **04 90 54 44 48**

Alpes-Maritimes

Nice

Galerie Ferrero

Exponents of the Nice School (► 80) – very modern and very expensive.

✉ **21 rue de France/2 rue du Congrés** ☎ **04 93 88 83 89/04 93 88 34 44**

Atelier Galerie Dury

Contemporary paintings, sculptures and reliefs of a nautical theme by award-winning artist Christian Dury.

✉ **31 rue Droite, Vieux Nice** ☎ **04 93 62 50 57** 🚌 **All buses**

Tourette J

Antique clocks, watches and musical boxes have been Monsieur Tourette's speciality for over 30 years.

✉ **17 rue Lépante** ☎ **04 93 92 92 88**

Specialist Shops

Vaucluse

Avignon
Papiers-Plumes
Papiers-Plumes sells beautiful pens, paper and desk objects for lovers of the art of letter writing.
✉ 45 rue Joseph-Vernet
☎ 04 90 82 68 77

Scenes Interieures
A beautiful yet affordable interior design and gift shop.
✉ 41 rue d'Amphoux ☎ 04 90 86 46 31

Ménerbes
La Vie est Belle
Sophisticated soft furnishings and designer gifts for the home and garden.
✉ rue de la Fontaine ☎ 04 90 72 36 87

Bouches-du-Rhône

Aix
Ciné Photo Provence
Photographic equipment, films and a quality development service.
✉ 20 rue Bédarrides ☎ 04 42 93 47 30

St-Rémy-en-Provence
Galerie Gérard Sioen
Browse through arty photos, framed pictures, posters and cards of Provence.
✉ 55 rue Carnot ☎ 04 90 92 36 47

Alpes-Maritimes

Antibes
Antibes Shipservices
Here you will find everything from 'boaty' keyrings to fashionable yachting gear.

✉ 12 boulevard Aquillon
☎ 04 93 34 68 00

Cannes
Geneviève Lethu
A delightful gift shop, crammed from floor to ceiling with original presents and home decorations.
✉ 6 rue Maréchal-Joffre
☎ 04 93 68 18 19

Mélonie
The most exquisite dried flower arrangements you are ever likely to see.
✉ 80 rue d'Antibes ☎ 04 93 68 60 60

Nice
L'Atelier des Jouets
A magical shop full of sturdy, educational toys and games made in wood, metal and cloth. Ideal for children's gifts.
✉ 1 place de l'Ancien-Sénat
☎ 04 93 13 09 60

Domaine Massa
Hidden in the steep, sun-soaked hills behind Nice, this old farm cultivates two distinctly Niçois products – carnations and *vin de Bellet* (▶ panel).
✉ 596 chemin de Crémat
☎ 04 93 37 80 02

Halogene
Trendy interior design store. Furniture, lighting and gift ideas.
✉ 21 rue de la Buffa ☎ 04 93 88 96 26

St-Paul-de-Vence
Le Coucou
The witty handmade ceramics on sale here make highly original presents.
✉ Place de l'Église ☎ 04 93 32 91 18

A Little-Known Wine
Few people know about the tiny AOC (*appellation d'origine contrôllée*) wine region of Bellet near Nice, largely because the majority of the 160,000 or so bottles produced each year never gets any further than the cellars of the Riviera's top restaurants. The full-bodied red, with its wild cherry bouquet, can be aged up to 30 years. The golden white wine is reminiscent of Chablis and locals swear the rosé is the best accompaniment to regional fish dishes.

Amusement Parks, Sports & Museums

Snow Fun

Many of Provence's larger ski resorts offer excellent facilities for families with children of all ages, and a variety of winter sports: ice skating, husky-mushing, tobogganing, horse-drawn sleigh rides. The family resort of Orcières-Merlettes has a crèche for children from nine months to six years, the Jardin des Neiges snow-fun kindergarten for children aged three and above, and children's skiing lessons. Serre Chevalier and Isola 2000 (▶ 115) offer similar facilities.

Bouches-du-Rhône

Aquacity

Children are happy to splash away countless hours in this aquatic paradise of pools and water games.

✉ 13240 Septemes-les-Vallons (off Aix–Marseille autoroute), Marseille ☎ 04 91 51 54 08 🕐 Jun to mid-Sep, 10–7

El Dorado City

A Wild West park with pony rides, shows and entertainment in the middle of the Provence garrigue. Good fun for adults as well as children.

✉ 13820 Ensuès la Redonne ☎ 04 42 79 86 90 🕐 Summer daily 10–7; winter Sun only 10–7

Massalia Théâtre

Language proves no barrier when children's favourite fairy tales come alive here (▶ 114).

✉ 41 rue Jobin, 3e, Marseille ☎ 04 95 04 95 70 🚍 49A, 49B

La Petite Provence

A typical, if a little idealised, Provençal village recreated in miniature, showing daily scenes at school, the market and in the café.

✉ Avenue de la Vallée-des-Baux, Paradou ☎ 04 90 54 35 75 🕐 Daily 10–9

Parc Zoologique la Barben

Modern zoo with spacious enclosures for elephants, giraffes, tigers and white rhinos. Picnic area and playground.

✉ Route D572, between Salon-de-Provence and Aix-en-Provence ☎ 04 90 55 19 12 🕐 10–6

Var and Haute-Provence

Aqualibre

Children's courses in kayaking and white-water rafting in a safe environment. Polyglot instructors. Children must be able to swim.

✉ Base Eau-Vive du Rioclar, 04340 Meolans-Revel ☎ 04 92 81 90 96 🕐 Course consists of five hour-long lessons

Luna Park

Some of the most exhilarating fairground rides in Europe.

✉ Gassin, Golfe de St-Tropez ☎ 04 94 56 35 64 🕐 Early Apr to late Jun, 8:30PM–1AM; late Jun to mid-Sep, 8:30PM–2AM; Sun, hols from 4PM

Orcières-Merlette Ski Resort

Family fun in the snow (▶ panel).

✉ Orcières-Merlette ☎ 04 92 55 89 89 (Tourist Office)

Village des Tortues

A fascinating one-hour tour of this remarkable 'village' with its 1,200 turtles and tortoises.

✉ 83590 Gonfaron (off Aix–Cannes autoroute) ☎ 04 94 78 26 41 🕐 Mar–Oct, daily 9AM–6PM

Alpes-Maritimes

Antibes Land

All ages enjoy this amusement park – its big wheel, roller coaster and even its bungee jumping!

✉ Route N7 (opposite Marineland), Antibes ☎ 04 93 95 23 03 🕐 Jun–Sep daily, 3PM–2AM

Formule Kart'in

Indoor go-karting circuit for children (aged 6 upwards)

and adults.

✉ 215 avenue Francis-Tonner (RN7), Cannes ☎ 04 93 47 88 88 🕐 Mon–Thu 5:30–00:30, Fri 5:30–1, Sat 3–1, Sun 2–1

Fun Kart

Go-karting for children and adults, just outside Grasse.

✉ Bar-sur-Loup (Route de Gourdon) ☎ 04 93 42 48 08 🕐 Daily 12–6; Jul–Aug, 12–midnight

Grottes de St-Cézaire

Fairytale world of rich red caves filled with 'musical' stalactites and stalagmites in magical shapes.

✉ St-Cézaire-sur-Siagne ☎ 04 93 60 22 35 🕐 Jan–Mar, Oct, Nov 2:30–5; Apr, May 2:30–5:30; Jun & Sep 10:30–12, 2–6; Jul, Aug 10:30–6:30. Closed Dec

Hippodrome

Spend a memorable family night out at the horse races.

✉ Hippodrome Cagnes, Cagnes-sur-Mer ☎ 04 92 02 44 44 🕐 Early Jul to end Aug, Mon, Wed, Fri from 8:30PM

Marineland

The greatest marine show in Europe (▶ panel).

✉ Route N7 (opposite Antibes Land), Antibes ☎ 04 93 33 82 72 🕐 Daily 10–4 (until midnight Jul, Aug)

Musée de l'Automobiliste

Older children enjoy visiting the unique, radiator-shaped car museum, with its large collection of old and new cars and footage of classic races.

✉ 772 chemin de Font-de-Currault, Mougins ☎ 04 93 69 27 80 🕐 Daily 10–7

Musée National

A huge collection of dolls dating from the 18th century to Barbie.

✉ 17 avenue Princesse-Grace, Monaco ☎ 0377 93 30 91 26 🕐 Oct–Easter, 10–12:15, 2:30–6:30; Easter–Sep, 10–6.30. Closed 1 Jan, 1 May, 19 Nov, 25 Dec

Musée Océanographique

Jacques Cousteau's world-famous aquarium and marine museum appeals to children of all ages (▶ 83).

✉ Avenue St-Martin, Monaco ☎ 0377 90 15 36 00 🕐 Oct–Mar 10–6; Apr–Jun, Sep 9:30–7; Jul, Aug 9:30–7:30

Les Terrasses de Fontvieille

Prince Rainier's impressive collections of model boats and vintage cars, a zoo – and even a McDonald's!

✉ Terraces de Fontfieille, Monaco ☎ Zoo 0377 93 25 18 31; naval museum 0377 92 05 28 48; classic car exhibition 0377 92 05 28 56 🕐 Telephone for details

Tiki III

See the bulls, horses and wild birds of the Camargue on a 1½-hour mini cruise by a paddle boat.

✉ D38, 1.5km from Saintes-Maries-de-la-Mer ☎ 04 90 97 81 68 🕐 Mid-Mar to mid-Nov: multiple departures daily. Phone for times

Visiobulle

Discover the underwater world of 'Millionaire's Bay' in a glass-bottomed boat. Reservations recommended.

✉ Embarcadère Courbet, Juan-les-Pins ☎ 04 93 67 02 11 🕐 Apr–Jun departures at 11, 1:30, 3 & 4:30; Jul, Aug at 9, 10:25, 11:50, 2, 3:25, 4:50 & 6:15; Sep at 11, 1:30, 3 & 4:30

Marineland

A wonderful world of performing sea lions, killer whales, dolphins, and close underwater encounters with sharks (safely, within a transparent tunnel!). Children love the Jungle des Papillons with exotic butterflies, huge, hairy spiders and other creepy-crawlies. Younger children enjoy the pony tours, face painting and stroking the animals at La Petite Ferme Provençale. Older children hurtle down the Aqua-Splash water slides and mum and dad try their hand at crazy-golf. All this and more at Marineland.

Casinos, Cinemas & Nightspots

The Man Who Broke the Bank!
The glitz of the Riviera's casinos are famous the world over, in particular the one at Monte-Carlo (► 82), where Charles Deville Wells turned $400 into $40,000 in a three-day gambling spree, thereby inspiring the song *The Man who Broke the Bank at Monte-Carlo*.

Vaucluse

Avignon
Bar Les Celestins
This tiny, brightly coloured bar draws a trendy crowd to its shady terrace for cocktails and barrelled beers.
✉ 38 place des Corps-Saints ☎ No telephone ⏰ 7AM–1AM

Peniche Dolphin Blues
A café-theatre on a barge moored on the Rhône near Avignon's bridge. Cabaret and live music most evenings and a children's theatre during the day.
✉ Chemin de l'Île-Piot ☎ 04 90 82 46 96

Utopia/Ajmi
Five screens showing original-version films, attached to Ajmi Jazz Club. Dance spectacles and cabaret.
✉ 4 rue Escaliers Ajmi ☎ 04 90 82 65 36 (Ajmi 04 90 86 08 61) ⏰ Films most days (phone for details). Jazz nights: Thu, Fri

Bouches-du-Rhône

Aix-en-Provence
Le Mistral
Join the locals for the latest sounds in techno, house and garage music. Overflowingly popular nightclub.
✉ 3 rue Fréderic-Mistral ☎ 04 42 38 16 49 ⏰ 11PM–6AM

Le Scat
A traditional club with live jazz, soul, rhythm and blues, and reggae.
✉ 11 rue de la Verrerie ☎ 04 42 23 00 23 ⏰ Tue–Sat 11PM–5AM

Arles
Café la Nuit
Popular meeting place at the heart of Arles and subject of a famous van Gogh painting.
✉ 11 place du Forum ☎ 04 90 49 83 30 ⏰ 9AM–midnight

Aubagne
Espace 'La Belle Époque'
Atmospheric bar-cum-café theatre with live music, cabaret and readings.
✉ 4 bis cours Foch ☎ 04 42 03 13 66 ⏰ 7:30PM–2AM

Marseille
Trolleybus
Marseille's number one rock venue. Three bars and two bowling alleys.
✉ 24 quai Rive-Neuve ☎ 04 91 54 30 45 ⏰ Tue–Sat 11:30PM–5AM (6 Sat, Sun); Tue–Wed (bar only) open until midnight 🚇 Metro (Vieux Port)

Stes-Maries-de-la-Mer
Bar-El Compo
Café with live entertainment and frequent flamenco shows.
✉ 13 rue Victor-Hugo ☎ 04 90 97 84 11 ⏰ 8AM–1AM. Show every Sat eve in summer

Var and Haute-Provence

St-Tropez
Les Caves du Roy
Reputedly St-Tropez' spiciest nightspot.
✉ Hôtel Byblos, avenue Paul-Signac ☎ 04 94 97 16 02 ⏰ Easter–Oct 11PM–5AM

VIP Room
This star-studded nightclub is the place to see and be seen.
✉ boulevard 11-Novembre 1918 ☎ 04 94 97 14 70 ⏰ Open weekends only in winter

Alpes-Maritimes

Antibes
La Siesta
One of the Côte d'Azur's most exotic nightclubs with open-air dance floors, fountains, flaming torches and a wave-shaped casino.

✉ **Route du Bord-de-la-Mer (between Antibes and la Brague)** ☎ **04 93 33 31 31** 🕐 **Mid-May to mid-Sep 11PM–4AM**

Cannes
Planet Hollywood
This popular bar, opened in May 1997 by Bruce Willis, Demi Moore, John Travolta and Sylvester Stallone, is currently one of *the* places to see and be seen.

✉ **1 les allées de la Libérté** ☎ **04 93 38 60 31** 🕐 **11:30–1AM**

Juan-les-Pins
Whiskey à Gogo
Join locals for the latest sounds in this popular nightclub.

✉ **rue Jacques Leonetti** ☎ **04 93 61 26 40** 🕐 **10PM–late summer only**

Monaco
Café de Paris
Even if you are not a big-spender you will be tempted by the dazzling array of slot machines in this famous café (▶ panel).

✉ **Place du Casino** ☎ **0377 92 16 20 20** 🕐 **All day from 10AM.**

Le Casino
The most famous, ritziest casino on the Riviera, but with an entrance fee.

✉ **Place du Casino** ☎ **0377 92 16 20 00** 🕐 **noon till dawn**

Cinema d'Été
An open-air cinema, summertime only.

✉ **Chemanded Pêcheurs** ☎ **0377 93 25 86 80**

Monte-Carlo
Jimmi'z
Join the jet set at the chicest disco on the Riviera.

✉ **26 avenue Princesse-Grace** ☎ **0377 92 16 22 77** 🕐 **11.30PM–around 5AM**

Nice
Casino Ruhl
Nice's glamorous casino offers spectacular dinner cabarets as well as private gaming rooms.

✉ **Promenade des Anglais** ☎ **04 97 03 12 22** 🕐 **10AM–5AM**

Cinémathèque
Classic films as well as the latest releases.

✉ **3 esplanade Kennedy** ☎ **04 92 04 06 66** 🕐 **Tel for details** 🚌 **All buses**

Le Grand Escurial
Nice's largest indoor nightclub draws crowds of all ages for its guest DJs and popular sounds, ranging from house to R&B. Free breakfast is served at 4AM.

✉ **29 rue Alphonse Karr** ☎ **04 93 82 37 66** 🕐 **Midnight–4.**

L'Iguane
An established Niçois nightspot on the old port, with tropical guerrilla decor.

✉ **5 quai des Deux-Emmanuel** ☎ **04 93 56 83 83** 🕐 **Daily 11:30PM–5AM** 🚌 **2, 9, 10**

Thor Pub
A lively tourist pub and pavement terrace on Nice's main market square. Live music 10PM-2AM nightly.

✉ **32 Cours Saleya** ☎ **04 93 62 49 90** 🕐 **6PM–2:30AM. Happy hour 6–8:30PM**

Café de Paris
This beautifully renovated art-deco triumph contains a restaurant as well as a gaming house, which in its heyday attracted the world's society. Ladies' man Edward VII was a frequent visitor, and the delicious dessert crêpe Suzette was created here, named after one of his companions.

Theatre, Opera & Classical Music

Nice's Acropolis
Love it or hate it, one thing is for sure – you can't ignore this monstrous mass of smoked glass and concrete slabs at the very hub of modern Nice. Nevertheless, with its four high-tech auditoria, concert hall, bowling alley, exhibition halls, Cinémathèque (► 113) and extensive conference facilities.

Ticket Sales

Avignon
FNAC
✉ 19 rue de la République
☎ 04 90 14 35 35

Marseille
FNAC
✉ Centre Commercial Borse
☎ 04 91 39 94 00

Virgin Megastore
✉ 75 rue St-Ferréol ☎ 04 91 55 55 00

Nice
FNAC
✉ Nice Etoile, 30 avenue Jean-Médecin ☎ 04 92 17 77 77

Vaucluse

Avignon
Opera Théâtre d'Avignon
Concerts by the Orchestra Lyrique de Région Avignon-Provence. Also ballet.
✉ 1 rue Racine
☎ 04 90 82 42 42

Théâtre du Chêne-Noir
Small theatre with a top repertory company.
✉ 8 bis rue Ste-Catherine
☎ 04 90 82 40 57

Orange
Théâtre Antique
Concerts, opera and theatre in an superb setting (► 26).
✉ Place des Frères-Mounet
☎ 04 90 51 17 60

Bouches-du-Rhône

Aix
Théâtre du Jeu de Paume
Aix's number one theatre and concert venue.
✉ 17 rue de l'Opera ☎ 04 42 99 12 00

Marseille
Massalia Théâtre
France's first marionnette theatre (► 110).
✉ 41 rue Jobin ☎ 04 95 04 95 70

L'Opéra de Marseille
Predominantly Italian opera. Roland Petit's famous National Ballet Company is also based here.
✉ 2 place Reyer ☎ 04 91 55 11 10 🚇 Metro (Vieux Port)

Theatre National de Marseille la Criée
Marseille's leading theatre, housed in a former fish auction house, giving widely acclaimed performances.
✉ 30 quai de Rive-Neuve, 7e
☎ 04 96 17 80 00 🚌 31 33, 34, 41, 80, 81

Alpes-Maritimes

Nice
L'Acropolis
This vast, modern congress, arts and tourism centre is popular for theatre, films and concerts (► panel).
✉ 1 esplanade Kennedy
☎ 04 93 92 83 00 🚌 All buses

Opéra de Nice
Home of the Nice Opera, the Philharmonic Orchestra and Ballet Corps, a rococo extravaganza in red and gold modelled on the Naples opera house.
✉ 4/6 rue St-François-de-Paule ☎ 04 92 17 40 00 🚌 All buses

Théâtre de Nice (TDN)
This modern theatre presents world-class shows.
✉ Promenade des Arts
☎ 04 93 13 90 90 🚌 All buses

Participatory Sports

Alpine skiing

Isola 2000
Day trips from Nice coach station include a ski pass.
☎ 04 93 23 15 15

Serre Chevalier
Provence's premier ski resort, near Briançon.
☎ 04 92 24 98 98

Ballooning

Montgolfière Provence
The ultimate way to explore the region.
✉ Joucas
☎ 04 90 05 76 77

Canoeing

Kayak Vert, Fontaine-de-Vaucluse
The scenic Sorgue river is a favourite venue for canoeing and kayaking enthusiasts.
✉ 84800 Fontaine-de-Vaucluse
☎ 04 90 52 56 56

Cross-Country Skiing

Gap Bayard
One of the largest *ski-de-fond* (cross-country skiing) regions in the Hautes-Alpes.
☎ 04 92 52 56 56

Deep-sea Fishing

Guigo Marine, Antibes
Tired of lazing on the beach? Book a day trip out at sea.
✉ 9 avenue 11-Novembre
☎ 04 93 34 17 17 ⊙ Jun–Oct

Golf

Royal Mougins Golf Club
To some, the best golf club on the Côte d'Azur.
✉ 424 avenue du Roi ☎ 04 92 92 49 69

Hang-gliding

The most popular areas are Mont Ventoux and the Lubéron.
✉ **Association Vaucluse Parapente, 26 rue des Teinturiers, Avignon** ☎ 04 90 85 67 82

River Cruises

Mireio, Avignon
Explore the Provençal waterways.
✉ Allée de l'Oulle ☎ 04 90 85 62 25

Sailing

Centre Nautique Municipal, Cannes
Hire and tuition in sailing dinghies, catamarans and windsurfing, for adults and children.
✉ Port du Mourre-Rouge
☎ 04 92 18 88 87

Scuba Diving

Fédération Française de Sports Sous-Marins, Marseille
The Riviera offers some of the finest diving in Europe.
✉ 24 quai Rive Neuve ⊙ 04 91 33 99 31

Tennis

Lawn Tennis Club, Nice
Venue of the Nice Open and former club of French tennis star, Yannick Noah.
✉ 5 avenue Suzanne-Lenguen
☎ 04 92 15 58 00

Yacht Charter

Moorings, Nice
Skippered yachts for hire.
✉ Quai Amiral-Infernet
☎ 04 92 00 42 22

Spectator Sports
The region's number one spectator sport is *le foot* (football) and its top team is Olympique de Marseille, (☎ 04 91 32 13 21 for tickets). In the Camargue area the most popular sport is bullfighting (► 50), but the Monte-Carlo Rally (Jan), Monaco's Formula One Grand Prix (May) and the Monte-Carlo and Nice Open Tennis Championships (Apr) are also huge crowd-pullers, along with regular horse racing at Cagnes and Marseilles.

All France is fanatical about cycling, with the Tour de France scaling some of Provence's highest mountain passes. Also, every summer crowds flock to Nice for its international triathlon (cycling, running, swimming) – the so-called 'Madman's Promenade'.

What's On When

Christmas Mass
Provençal midnight mass takes place at Aix, les Baux, Fontvieille, St-Rémy, Séguret, Tarascon

January
Monte-Carlo Rally (➤ 115)
Monte-Carlo International Circus Festival

February
Nice Carnival (2 weeks, ➤ 60–1)
Fête du Citron, Menton (10 days ➤ 60)
Corso du Mimosa, Bormes-les-Mimosas (10 Feb, ➤ 68)

March
Dance Festival, Cannes

April
International Tennis Open, Nice and Monte-Carlo
Ski Grand Prix, Isola 2000
Wine-growers' Festival, Châteauneuf-du-Pape (25 Apr)
Easter Festival and start of bullfighting season, Arles (4 days at Easter)
Fête des Gardians, Arles (last Sunday, ➤ 60)

May
Cannes Film Festival (2nd week, ➤ 85, 60)
Fête de la Rose, Grasse (2nd weekend)
Bravade de St-Torpes, St-Tropez (16–17 May, ➤ 66)
International Formula One Grand Prix, Monaco
Ochre Festival, Roussillon (Ascension weekend)
Gypsy Pilgrimage, Stes-Maries-de-la-Mer (24–5 May, ➤ 57)

June
Dance, music and folklore festival, Arles
Jazz Festival, Aix
Sacred Music Festival, Nice
Fête de la Tarasque, Tarascon (last Sun, ➤ 58)

July
Nice Jazz Festival (first 2 weeks)

International Folklore Festival, Marseille (first 2 weeks)
Rencontres Internationales de la Photographie, Arles
International Music Festival, Aix (last 3 weeks, ➤ 60)
Annual Provençal Boules Competition, Marseille (mid-Jul)
Chorègies Music Festival, Orange (last 2 weeks)
Food Festival, Carpentras (3rd weekend)
International Art Festival, Cagnes
International Theatre Festival Avignon (mid-Jul to mid-Aug)
International Fireworks Festival, Monaco (Jul–Aug)
Numerous arts festivals at Arles, Gordes, Fontaine-de-Vaucluse, Menton, Sisteron, St-Paul-de-Vence, Vaison-la Romaine, Vence and other towns and villages (Jul/Aug)

August
Grape-ripening Festival, Châteauneuf-du-Pape (1st weekend, ➤ 60)
Lavender Festival, Digne
Fête de St-Laurent, Eygalières (9–11 Aug, ➤ 56)

September
Rice Harvest Festival and end of bullfighting season, Arles (2nd Sun)
Les Voiles de St-Trpez Yacht Regatta (End Sep–1st week Oct)

October
International Folklore Fair, Marseille

November
Santon Fair, Marseille (last Sun–Epiphany)

Practical Matters

Above: Mardi
Gras time in
Nice
Right: pastis
from Marseille

TIME DIFFERENCES

GMT 12 noon	France 1PM	Germany 1PM	USA (NY) 7AM	Netherlands 1PM	Spain 1PM

BEFORE YOU GO

WHAT YOU NEED

● Required
○ Suggested
▲ Not required

Some countries require a passport to remain valid for a minimum period (usually at least six months) beyond the date of entry – contact their consulate or embassy or your travel agent for details.

	UK	Germany	USA	Netherlands	Spain
Passport/National Identity Card	●	●	●	●	●
Visa (Regulations can change – check before your journey)	▲	▲	▲	▲	▲
Onward or Return Ticket	▲	▲	▲	▲	▲
Health Inoculations	▲	▲	▲	▲	▲
Health Documentation (reciprocal agreement document) (▶ 123, Health)	●	●	▲	●	●
Travel Insurance	○	○	○	○	○
Driving Licence (national)	●	●	●	●	●
Car Insurance Certificate (if own car)	○	●	○	○	○
Car Registration Document (if own car)	●	●	●	●	●

WHEN TO GO

Provence/Côte d'Azur

High season

Low season

12°C	12°C	14°C	18°C	21°C	27°C	28°C	28°C	25°C	22°C	17°C	14°C
JAN	FEB	MAR	APR	MAY	JUN	JUL	AUG	SEP	OCT	NOV	DEC

Very wet   Wet   Cloud   Sun

TOURIST OFFICES

In the UK

French Government Tourist Office
178 Piccadilly
London W1J 9AL
☎ 0891 244123
(recorded information)

Monaco Tourist Convention Office
206 Harbour Yard,
Chelsea Harbour
London SW10 0XD
☎ 0500 006114 and
0207 352 99 62

In the USA

French Government Tourist Office
444 Madison Avenue, 16th floor
New York. NY10022
☎ 212/838 7800

Monaco Government Tourist Bureau
565 Fifth Avenue,
23rd floor, New York NY10017
☎ 212/286 3330

POLICE 17

FIRE 18

AMBULANCE 15

SOS TRAVELLERS 04 91 62 12 80

WHEN YOU ARE THERE

ARRIVING

The national airline, Air France (☎ 0820 820 820 in France). has scheduled flights from Britain, mainland Europe and beyond, to Marseille and Nice. French Railways (SNCF) operate high speed trains (TGV) from Paris to main Provence and Côte d'Azur stations.

Marseille-Provence Airport Journey times
Kilometres to city centre

25 kilometres

🚇	N/A
🚌	25 minutes
🚗	30 minutes

Nice-Côte d'Azur Airport Journey times
Kilometres to city centre

7 kilometres

🚇	N/A
🚌	20 minutes
🚗	15 minutes

MONEY

The euro is the official currency of France and Monaco. Euro banknotes and coins were introduced in January 2002. Banknotes are in denominatins of 5, 10, 20, 50, 100, 200 and 500 euros and coins are in denominations of 1, 2, 5, 10, 20 and 50 cents, and 1 and 2 euros. Euro traveller's cheques are widely accepted as are major credit cards. Credit and debit cards can also be used for withdrawing euro notes from cash machines which are widely accessible. France and Monaco's former currency, the French franc, went out of circulation in early 2002.

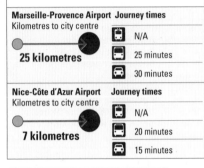

TIME

🕐 France is one hour ahead of Greenwich Mean Time (GMT+1). From late March, when clocks are put forward one hour, until late October, French summer time (GMT +2) operates.

CUSTOMS

➜ **YES**
From another EU country for personal use (guidelines)
800 cigarettes, 200 cigars, 1 kilogram of tobacco
10 litres of spirits (over 22%)
20 litres of aperitifs
90 litres of wine, of which 60 litres can be sparkling wine
110 litres of beer

From a non-EU country for your personal use, the allowances are:
200 cigarettes OR
50 cigars OR
250 grams of tobacco
1 litre of spirits (over 22%)
2 litres of intermediary products (eg sherry) and sparkling wine
2 litres of still wine
50 grams of perfume
0.25 litres of eau de toilette

The value limit for goods is 175 euros

Travellers under 17 years of age are not entitled to the tobacco and alcohol allowances.

➊ **NO**
Drugs, firearms, ammunition, offensive weapons, obscene material, unlicensed animals.

119

CONSULATES

UK	Germany	USA	Netherlands	Spain
04 91 15 72 10 (Mar)	04 91 16 75 20 (Mar)	04 91 54 92 00 (Mar)	04 91 25 66 64 (Mar)	377 93 30 24 98 (M)
04 93 62 13 56 (N)	04 93 83 55 25 (N)	04 93 88 89 55 (N)	04 93 87 52 94 (N)	
377 93 50 99 54 (M)	377 97 77 51 53 (M)		377 92 05 15 02 (M)	

Key: (Mar) - Marseille (N) - Nice (M) - Monaco

WHEN YOU ARE THERE

TOURIST OFFICES

Provence and Côte d'Azur
● Comité Régional de Tourisme Provence-Alpes-Côte-d'Azur
Les Docks
10 place de la Joliette,
13567 Marseille
☎ 04 91 56 47 00
Fax 04 91 56 47 01

Département Offices
● Comité Régional de Tourisme Rivièra Côte d'Azur
55 promenade des Anglais
BP 602, 06011 Nice
☎ 04 93 37 78 78
Fax 04 93 86 01 06

● Comité Départemental du Tourisme des Bouches-du-Rhône
Le Montesquieu
13 rue Roux de Brignoles
13006 Marseille
☎ 04 91 13 84 13
Fax 04 91 33 01 82

● Comité Départemental du Tourisme du Vaucluse
12 rue College-de-la-Croix
BP147, 84008 Avignon
☎ 04 90 80 47 00
Fax 04 90 86 86 08

Monaco
● Office National du Tourisme de la Principauté de Monaco
2a boulevard des Moulins
Monte-Carlo
MC 98030 Monaco
☎ 377 92 16 61 66
Fax 377 92 16 60 00

Look for 🛈 in the gazetteer for information in other towns and villages.

NATIONAL HOLIDAYS

J	F	M	A	M	J	J	A	S	O	N	D
2		(2)	(2)	3(4)	1(2)	1	1			3	2

1 Jan	New Year's Day
27 Jan	St Devote's Day (Monaco only)
Mar/Apr	Easter Sunday and Monday
1 May	Labour Day
8 May	VE Day (France only)
May/Jun	Whit Sunday and Monday
June	Corpus Christi (Monaco only)
14 July	Bastille Day (France only)
15 Aug	Assumption
1 Nov	All Saints' Day
11 Nov	Remembrance Day (France only)
19 Nov	Monaco National Holiday (Monaco only)
9 Dec	Immaculate Conception (Monaco only)
25 Dec	Christmas Day

OPENING HOURS

○ Shops	● Restaurants
● Offices	○ Museums/Monuments
● Banks	○ Pharmacies

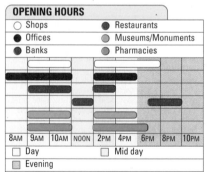

| 8AM | 9AM | 10AM | NOON | 2PM | 4PM | 6PM | 8PM | 10PM |

☐ Day	☐ Mid day
☐ Evening	

In addition to the times shown above, afternoon time of shops in summer is 4 to 8 or 9PM. Most shops close Sunday and many on Monday. Small food shops open from 7AM and may open Sunday morning. Large department stores do not close for lunch and hyper-markets open 10AM to 9 or 10PM but may shut Monday morning. Banks are closed Sunday as well as Saturday or Monday.

Museums and monuments have extended summer hours. Many close one day a week; either Monday (municipal ones) or Tuesday (national ones):

120

DRIVE ON THE RIGHT

TOILETS CHARGE ★★ ★★

PUBLIC TRANSPORT

 Internal Flights Air Inter – information via Air France (▶ 119, **Arriving**) and travel agents – is the French internal airline, linking 45 cities and towns, among them Marseille, Toulon, Avignon, Nîmes, Nice, Cannes and Fréjus. Some private airlines serve smaller towns.

 Trains The main line in Provence and the Côte d'Azur links the towns and cities of the coast with the Rhône valley, with Marseille as its hub. A spectacular stretch runs behind the coast from Fréjus/St-Raphaël to Menton, which in summer is the most efficient way to move along the coast.

 Area Buses Services run by a number of private companies are punctual and comfortable, but not very frequent outside main urban areas and coastal resorts. There are also SNCF buses which serve places on rail routes where trains do not stop. Bus stations: Marseille (☎ 04 91 08 16 40); Nice (☎ 04 93 85 61 81)

 Island Ferries There are ferries to the three islands off the coast of Hyères: the Îles d'Hyères (Porquerolles, Port-Cros, and Île de Levant) from five ports along the Côte d'Azur (Cavalaire, le Lavandou, Hyères-Plage, Toulon and la Tour-Fondue). Some services operate summer only.

 Urban Transport Most sizeable towns have a bus station (*gare routière*), often near the railway station. Services, even in cities, stop about 9PM. The most efficient bus network is in Nice, where computerised signboards at every bus stop inform you of the exact time of arrival of your service.

CAR RENTAL

 All the main car-rental companies have desks at Marseille and Nice airports and in main towns. Car hire is expensive, but airlines and tour operators offer fly-drive, and French Railways (SNCF) train-car packages, often more economical than hiring locally.

TAXIS

 Taxis are very expensive and not allowed to cruise. They must pick up at ranks (*stations de taxi*) found at airports, railway stations and elsewhere. Always check there is a meter. There is a pick-up charge plus a rate per minute – check with the driver.

DRIVING

 Speed limits on toll motorways: **130kph (110kph** when wet); non-toll motorways and dual carriageways: **110kph (100kph** when wet). In fog (visibility less than 50m): **50kph** all roads

 Speed limits on country roads: **90kph (80kph** when wet)

 Speed limits on urban roads: **50kph** (limit starts at town sign)

 Must be worn in front seats at all times and in rear seats where fitted.

 Random breath-testing is frequent. Never drive under the influence of alcohol.

 Petrol (*essence*), including unleaded (*sans plomb*), and diesel are widely available. Petrol stations are numerous along main roads but rarer in mountainous areas. Some on minor roads are closed on Sundays. Maps showing petrol stations are available from main tourist offices.

A red warning triangle must be carried if your car has no hazard warning lights, but it is advised for all motorists. Place this 30m behind the car in the event of an accident or breakdown. On motorways ring from emergency phones (every 2km) to contact the breakdown service. Off motorways, police will advise on local breakdown services.

PERSONAL SAFETY

The Police Municipale (blue uniforms) carry police duties in cities and towns. The Gendarmes (blue trousers, black jackets, white belts), the national police force, cover the countryside and smaller places. The CRS deal with emergencies and also look after safety on beaches. Monaco has its own police.

To avoid danger or theft:
- Do not use unmanned roadside rest areas at night.
- Cars, especially foreign cars, shoud be secured.
- Beware of pickpockets.

Police assistance:
☎ **17**
from any call box

ELECTRICITY

The local power supply is: 220 volts

Type of socket:
Round two-hole sockets taking two-round-pin (or

occasionally three-round-pin plugs. British visitors should

bring an adaptor; US visitors a voltage transformer.

TELEPHONES

All telephone numbers in France comprise ten digits (eight in Monaco). There are no area codes except for Monaco (377 precedes number when phoning from outside the principality). Most public phones use a phone card (*télécartes*), sold in units of 50 or 120 in post offices, tobacconists and newsagents.

International Dialling Codes

From France and Monaco to:	
UK:	00 44
Germany:	00 49
USA:	00 1
Netherlands:	00 31
Spain:	00 34

POST

Post Offices
The PTT (*Poste et Télécommunications*) deals with mail and telephone services. Outside main centres, post offices open shorter hours and may close 12–2. Letter boxes are yellow. ⏰ 8–7 (12 Sat), closed Sun
☎ 04 91 15 47 00 (Marseille)
☎ 04 93 82 65 00 (Nice)

TIPS/GRATUITIES

Yes ✓ No ✗		
Restaurants (service incl; tip optional)	✗	
Cafés (service included; tip optional)	✗	
Hotels (service included; tip optional)	✗	
Hairdressers	✓	(1 euro)
Taxis	✓	(1 euro)
Tour guides	✓	(1 euro)
Cinema usherettes	✓	(30c)
Porters	✓	(1 euro)
Cloakroom attendants	✓	(15–30c)
Toilets	✓	(cents)

PHOTOGRAPHY

What to photograph: From the snow-peaked lower Alps to the Grand Cañon of central Provence and the *calanques* (narrow coastal inlets). The bright Provence light further enhances the beauty of the landscape.

Where to buy film: The most popular brands and types of film can be bought from shops and photo laboratories. Film development is quite expensive.

Restrictions: Some museums will allow you to photograph inside. In churches with frescoes and icons, prior permission for flashlight is required.

HEALTH

Insurance
EU nationals can obtain medical treatment at reduced cost on production of a qualifying form (Form E111 for Britons); however this does not apply to Monaco. Private medical insurance is still advisable for all visitors to France.

Dental Services
As for general medical treatment (➤ above, **Insurance**), nationals of EU countries can obtain dental treatment at reduced cost. Around 70 per cent of dentists' standard fees are refunded. Private medical insurance is still advisable for all.

Sun Advice
The sunshine yearly average is 2,500 hours, rising to 3,000 hours along the coast. Summers, particularly July and August, are dry and hot. If walking, wear a hat and drink plenty of fluids. On the beach, a high-protection sunblock is a must.

Drugs
Pharmacies – recognised by their green cross sign – possess highly qualified staff able to offer medical advice, provide first aid and prescribe and provide a wide range of drugs, though some are available by prescription (*ordonnance*) only.

Safe Water
It is safe to drink tap water served in hotels and restaurants, but never drink from a tap marked *eau non potable*. Many prefer the taste of bottled water which is cheap and widely available.

CONCESSIONS

Students/Youths A youth card (*Carte Jeune*), available to those under 26, entitles holders to various discounts on public transport, museum admissions, entertainments, shopping and other facilities (including meals in university canteens); ask at tourist offices and post offices for details.

Senior Citizens A number of tour companies offer special arrangements for senior citizens; for further information contact the French Government Tourist Office (➤ 118, **Tourist Offices**). Senior citizens (aged over 60) are eligible for reduced or free entrance to sights, and if aged over 65 are eligible for fare discounts on public transport.

CLOTHING SIZES

France	UK	Rest of Europe	USA		
46	36	46	36		
48	38	48	38		
50	40	50	40		
52	42	52	42		Suits
54	44	54	44		
56	46	56	46		
41	7	41	8		
42	7½	42	8½		
43	8½	43	9½		
44	9½	44	10½		Shoes
45	10½	45	11½		
46	11	46	12		
37	14½	37	14½		
38	15	38	15		
39/40	15½	39/40	15½		
41	16	41	16		Shirts
42	16½	42	16½		
43	17	43	17		
36	8	34	6		
38	10	36	8		
40	12	38	10		
42	14	40	12		Dresses
44	16	42	14		
46	18	44	16		
38	4½	38	6		
38	5	38	6½		
39	5½	39	7		
39	6	39	7½		Shoes
40	6½	40	8		
41	7	41	8½		

WHEN DEPARTING

- Contact the airport or airline on the day prior to leaving to ensure that the flight details are unchanged.
- Expect to pay an airport departure tax (usually already included in the price of your flight ticket).
- Check the duty-free limits of the country you are entering before departure.

LANGUAGE

French is the native language. In Monaco the traditional Monégasque language (a mixture of French, Provençal and Italian Ligurian) is spoken by the older generation. English is spoken by those involved in tourism and in the larger cosmopolitan centres – less so in smaller, rural places. However, attempts to speak French will always be appreciated. Below is a list of a few helpful words.
More extensive coverage can be found in the AA's Essential *French Phrase Book*.

🛏	hotel	*l'hôtel*	rate	*le tarif*
	room	*la chambre*	breakfast	*le petit déjeuner*
	single room	*une personne*	toilet	*les toilettes*
	double room	*deux personnes*	bathroom	*une salle de bain*
	per person	*par personne*	shower	*une douche*
	per room	*par chambre*	key	*la clé*
	one/two nights	*une/deux nuits*	chambermaid	*la femme de*
	reservation	*une réservation*		*chambre*
💱	bank	*une banque*	banknote	*un billet*
	exchange office	*un bureau de change*	change	*la monnaie*
			credit card	*une carte de crédit*
	post office	*la poste*		
	foreign exchange	*le change extérieur*	traveller's cheque	*un chèque de voyage*
	British pound	*la livre sterling*	exchange rate	*le taux de change*
	American dollar	*le dollar*	commission	*la commission*
🍴	restaurant	*le restaurant*	starter	*le hors d'oeuvres*
	café	*la café*	main course	*le plat principal*
	table	*une table*	dish of the day	*le plat du jour*
	menu	*le menu*	dessert	*le dessert*
	set menu	*le menu du jour*	drink(s)	*une (les) boisson*
	wine list	*la carte des vins*	waiter	*le garçon*
	lunch	*le déjeuner*	waitress	*la serveuse*
	dinner	*le dîner*	the bill	*l'addition*
🚌	aeroplane	*l'avion*	ticket	*un billet*
	airport	*l'aéroport*	single/return	*simple/retour*
	train	*le train*	ticket office	*le guichet*
	train station	*la gare*	timetable	*l'horaire*
	bus	*l'autobus*	seat	*une place*
	bus station	*la gare routière*	non smoking	*non-fumeurs*
	ferry/boat	*le bateau*	reserved	*réservée*
	port	*le port*	window	*la fenêtre*
💬	yes	*oui*	tomorrow	*demain*
	no	*non*	yesterday	*hier*
	please	*s'il vous-plaît*	how much?	*combien?*
	thank you	*merci*	too expensive	*trop cher*
	hello	*bonjour*	open	*ouvert*
	goodbye	*au revoir*	closed	*fermé*
	good evening	*bonsoir*	second class	*deuxième classe*
	sorry	*pardon*	first class	*première classe*
	excuse me	*excusez-moi*	you're welcome	*de rien/avec plaisir*
	help!	*au secours!*	okay	*d'accord*
	today	*aujourd'hui*	I don't know	*Je ne sais pas*

INDEX

Acknowledgements
The Automobile Association wishes to thank the following libraries, photographers and associations for their assistance in the preparation of this book:
THE BRIDGEMAN ART LIBRARY, LONDON 22 The Rocaille Armchair, 1946 by Henri Matisse (1869–1954) Musée Matisse, Nice-Cimiez
MARY EVANS PICTURE LIBRARY 11
THE RONALD GRANT ARCHIVE 86
ROBERT HARDING PICTURE LIBRARY 15a, 16, 21, 77
MAGNUM PHOTOS LTD 14 (Eve Arnold)
M R I BANKERS' GUIDE TO FOREIGN CURRENCY 119
PICTURES COLOUR LIBRARY 62, 85
SPECTRUM COLOUR LIBRARY 122b
WORLD PICTURES 1

The remaining pictures are from the Association's own library (AA PHOTO LIBRARY) with contributions from:
ADRIAN BAKER 9c, 15b, 18, 19, 20, 23, 24/5, 26, 27a, 31, 32, 33, 35, 38, 40, 41, 44, 46, 49, 55, 59, 61b, 63, 67, 71b, 76, 82, 87, 88, 91a; PAUL KENWARD 47; ROB MOORE 6, 79; ROGER MOSS 122a, 122c; TONY OLIVER 68; NEIL RAY 60, 117a; KEV REYNOLDS 13; BARRIE SMITH 27b, 28/9, 66, 71a, 73, 74; RICK STRANGE 2, 5a, 5b, 7, 8a, 8b, 9a, 9b, 12a, 12b, 17, 34, 36a, 36b, 37, 39, 42, 43, 45, 48, 50, 52, 57, 58, 61a, 64, 65, 78, 80, 81, 89, 90, 91b, 117b

Author's Acknowledgements
Teresa Fisher wishes to thank the following for their assisatnce: the Tourist Boards of the Vaucluse, Bouches du Rhône and the Var; Nice Tourist Office; Hôtel Hi, Nice; Mas de la Beaume, Gordes; Domaine de Bournereau, Mouteux; Hôtel les Ateliers de l'Image, St-Rémy-de-Provence; la Maison du Monde, Cogolin, and the Four Seasons Provence at Terre Blanche.

Contributors
Copy editor: Penny Phenix Page Layout: Design 23 Verifier: David Hancock
Researcher (Practical Matters): Colin Follett Indexer: Marie Lorimer
Revision management: Pam Stagg

Dear Essential Traveller

Your comments, opinions and recommendations are very important to us. So please help us to improve our travel guides by taking a few minutes to complete this simple questionnaire.

You do not need a stamp (unless posted outside the UK). If you do not want to cut this page from your guide, then photocopy it or write your answers on a plain sheet of paper.

Send to: **The Editor, AA World Travel Guides, FREEPOST SCE 4598, Basingstoke RG21 4GY.**

Your recommendations...

We always encourage readers' recommendations for restaurants, nightlife or shopping – if your recommendation is used in the next edition of the guide, we will send you a *FREE* AA *Essential* Guide of your choice. Please state below the establishment name, location and your reasons for recommending it.

_____

_____

_____

_____

Please send me **AA *Essential*** _____

About this guide...

Which title did you buy?
    AA *Essential* _____

Where did you buy it? _____

When? m m / y y

Why did you choose an AA *Essential* Guide? _____

_____

_____

_____

_____

Did this guide meet your expectations?
    Exceeded ☐ Met all ☐ Met most ☐ Fell below ☐

Please give your reasons _____

_____

_____

_____

continued on next page...

Were there any aspects of this guide that you particularly liked? _____

_____

_____

Is there anything we could have done better? _____

_____

_____

About you...

Name (*Mr/Mrs/Ms*) _____

Address _____

_____

_____ Postcode _____

Daytime tel nos _____

Please only give us your mobile phone number if you wish to hear from us
about other products and services from the AA and partners by text or mms.

Which age group are you in?
Under 25 ☐   25–34 ☐   35–44 ☐   45–54 ☐   55–64 ☐   65+ ☐

How many trips do you make a year?
Less than one ☐   One ☐   Two ☐   Three or more ☐

Are you an AA member? Yes ☐   No ☐

About your trip...

When did you book? m m / y y   When did you travel? m m / y y

How long did you stay? _____

Was it for business or leisure? _____

Did you buy any other travel guides for your trip?

If yes, which ones? _____

Thank you for taking the time to complete this questionnaire. Please send it to us as soon as
possible, and remember, you do not need a stamp (*unless posted outside the UK*).

Happy Holidays!

Motorway with junction - Toll	Autobahn mit Anschlussstelle - Mautstelle
Motorway under construction - projected	Autobahn in Bau - geplant
Filling station - Restaurant - with motel	Tankstelle - Rasthaus - mit Motel
Road with four lanes - under construction	Vierspurige Straße - in Bau
Trunk road - under construction	National- oder Staatsstraße - in Bau
Important main road - under construction	Wichtige Hauptstraße - in Bau
Main road - Secondary road	Hauptstraße - Nebenstraße
Other road - Footpath	Fahrweg - Fußweg
Mountain pass closed in winter - Gradient	Passstraße mit Wintersperre - Steigung
Not suitable for caravans - closed	Für Wohnwagen nicht empfehlenswert - gesperrt
Toll road - Road closed for motor traffic	Gebührenpflichtige Straße - Für Kfz gesperrt
Main railway with station - Other railway	Hauptbahn mit Bahnhof - Nebenbahn
Railway (freight haulage) - Railway ferry for cars	Eisenbahn (Güterverkehr) - Autoverladung
Rack railway - Cable lift - Chair lift	Zahnradbahn - Seilbahn - Sessellift
Car ferry - Shipping route	Autofähre - Schifffahrtslinie
Airport - Regional airport - Airfield - Gliding field	Flughafen - Regionalflughafen - Flugplatz - Segelflugplatz
Place of particular interest	Besonders sehenswerter Ort
Natural object of particular interest	Besondere Natursehenswürdigkeit
Other objects of interest	Sonstige Sehenswürdigkeit
Scenic road	Landschaftlich schöne Strecke
Tourist route	Touristenstraße
National park, nature park - Viewpoint	Nationalpark, Naturpark - Aussichtspunkt
Botanical gardens, interesting park - Zoological garden	Botanischer Garten, sehenswerter Park - Zoologischer Garten
Castle open to public - Ruin	Burg, Schloss für Besucher zugänglich - Ruine
Other castle - Church - Monastery - Ruins	Sonstige Burg, Schloss - Kirche - Kloster - Ruinen
Hotel, motel, inn - Mountain hut - Tourist colony	Hotel, Motel, Gasthaus - Berghütte - Feriendorf
Camping - Youth hostel	Campingplatz - Jugendherberge
Bathing place - Swimming pool - Spa	Strandbad - Schwimmbad - Heilbad
State boundary	Staatsgrenze
International checkpoint - Checkpoint with restrictions	Grenzkontrollstelle international - mit Beschränkung
Administrative boundary - Restricted area	Verwaltungsgrenze - Sperrgebiet

Text labels within the legend graphics: Horb, Date/Datum, La Macchia, X-IV, 10%, MARSEILLE, Grotta d. Vento, Cittadella, Route des Grandes Alpes

130-137	0 — 5 km 0 — 3 miles	142-143	0 — 5 km 0 — 3 miles

Maps © Mairs Geographischer Verlag / Falk Verlag, 73751 Ostfildern

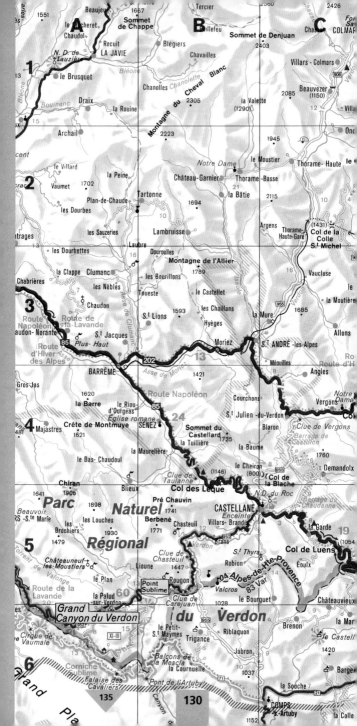

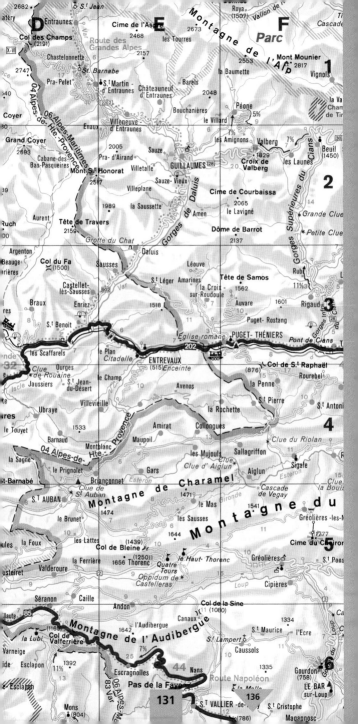

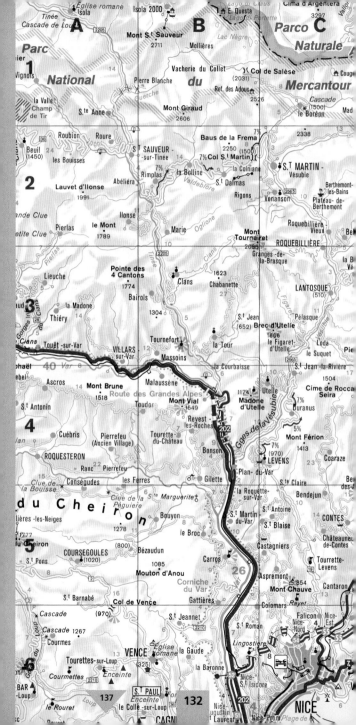

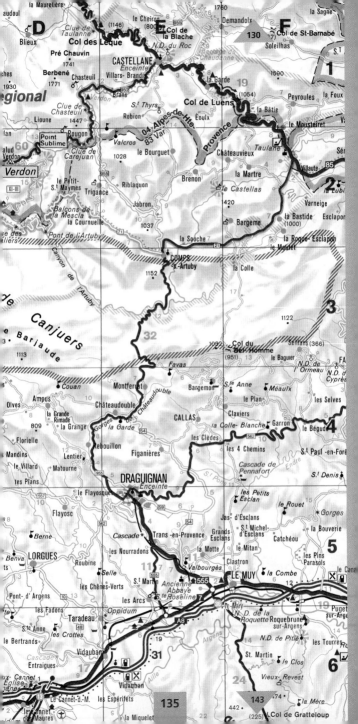

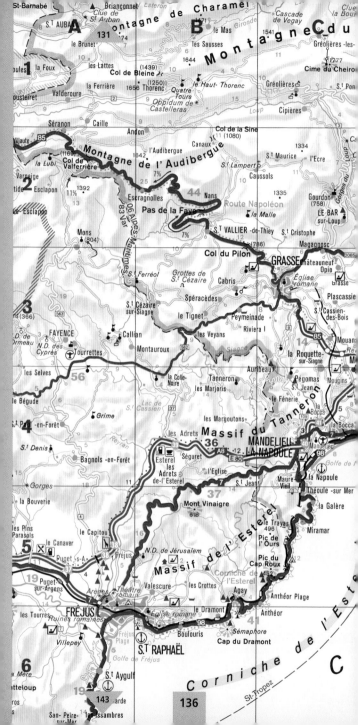

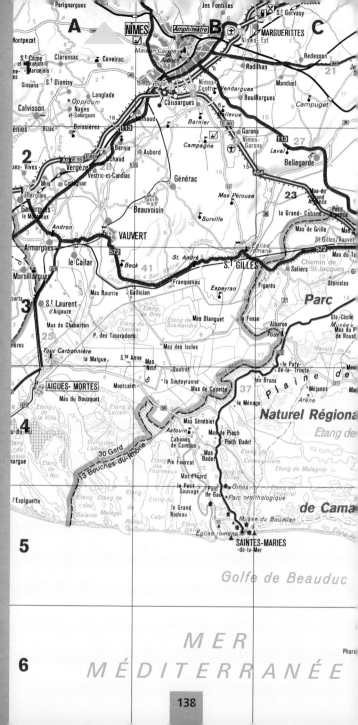

Parignargues
Les Fontilles
St Gervasy

A
NÎMES
Amphithéâtre
B
MARGUERITTES
C

Montpezat
Nîmes-Est
Redessan

St Côme
et-Maruéjols
Clarensac
Caveirac
Maison Carrée
Arènes
Rodilhan
Jo

Nîmes-
Maruéjols
St Dionisy
Manduel

Sinsans
Langlade
Nîmes-Ouest
Nîmes-
Centre
Vendargues
Bouillargues
Campuget

Calvisson
Oppidum
Nages
et-Solorgues
Caissargues
Bellevue

Boissières
Milhaud
Barnier
Garons
Nîmes-
Garons
113 27

Bizac
Bernis
Aubord
Campagne
A54
Laval
Bellegarde

Vives
Vergèze
Chaud
Vestric-et-Candiac
23
Mas du
Grand
Aunence
Petit
Aunence

Mus
Codognan
Générac
Mas Pérouse
la Grand- Cabane

Gallargues
Andron
Beauvoisin
Surville
Mas de Grille
St-Gilles/Vauver

Aimargues
VAUVERT
Église
Romane
572

le Cailar
Beck
41
St André
St GILLES
Chemin de
Saliers /St-Jacques

Marsillargues
Canal du 4 Bas-Rhône
Franquevau
Espeyran
Figarès
Stanislas

Mas Bourrie
Gallician
Parc

St Laurent
d'Aigouze
Étang
de Grey
Étang de
Scamandre
Mas Blanguet
la Fosse
Albaron
Tour
Ste-Cécile
Musée
Mas du P
de Roust

Mas de Chaberton
25
P. des Touradons
Mas des Iscles
le Paty-
de-la-Trinité

Tour Carbonnière
la Malgue
Ste Anne
Mas
Neuf
Quatret
es Bruns
Méjanes

AIGUES- MORTES
Montcalm
la Souteyranne
Mas de Capette
37
le Ménage
Plaine
Arène

Mas du Bousquet
Naturel Région

Étang de
la Ville
Étang des
Lairan
Mas Sénébier
le Pioch
Étang de

u-du-Roi
Astouin
Mas de Pioch
Pioch Badet

Étang
du Roi
Cabanes
de Cambon
30 Gard
113 Bouches-du-Rhône
Pin Fourcat
Mas
Badet
Étang de
Consecanière
Étang de Malagroy

l'Espiguette
Mas d'Icard
le Petit
Sauvage
Pont
de Gau
Ginès
Parc ornithologique
de Cama

Église romane
Musée du Boumian
SAINTES-MARIES
-de-la-Mer

Golfe de Beauduc

MER
MÉDITERRANÉE
Phare

138

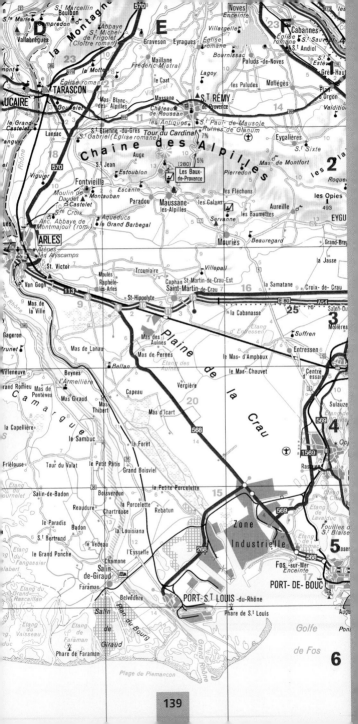

A Grand-Brays · Richebois · S.t Martin · Salon-Nord · Vernègues · **II** · Tallades · 25 · S.t Estèv Jans·

la Jasse · Salon-Nord · Aurons · Badasset · Temple romain · Aiguebelle · **Chaîne de la Tr** · Rognes · **C**

Croix- de- Crau · **SALON-de-Provence** · Vestiges antiques · Pélissanne · LAMBESC · Brest· · S.t Cannat · B

1 · Salon-Oubst · Mollères · Grans · Salon-Sud · la Barben · Barben · Valmousse · Autoroute du Soleil · TGV · **18** · Lignas S.

MIRAMAS · le Pont-du-Raud · Lançon-Provence · Caseneuve · les Quatre-Termes · Camaisse · les Gerv

Enceinte Miramas-le-Vieux · Confoux · Corpillon-Confoux · Lançon P.ce · Coudoux · Vestiges antiques · les Figons · Eguilles · Bompard

2 · S.t CHAMAS · Calissanne · les Baisses · la Fare-les-Oliviers · Coudoux · La Provencale · les 4 Tours · Ventabren · **19** · Gallice · les Mil

Sulauze · Pont Flavien (Flavius) · Oppidum du Castellan · la Bosque · Mauran · S.t Estève · **37** · **113** · Berre · **Chaîne de Vi** · Aqueduc de Roquefavour · la Mérindolle · le Petit Arboi · la Tour d' Arboi

ISTRES · Port des Heures Claires · Bouquet · la Suzanne · Raff SHELL · BERRE-l'Etang · **20** · Rognac · Velaux · Lenfa · Calas

Etang · **14** · Varage · Massane · Etang de Vaine · Vitrolles · Vitrolles · Montréon · les Champosse · **18** · Gardanne · Cabries · Plan de Campagne

de · S.t Mitre -les-Remparts · Fouilles de S.t Blaise · Roseron · Marseille (Provence) · MARIGNANE · S.t Victoret · les Plaines d'Arbois · les Pinchinades · Marignane-Ville · les Pennes · S.t Victoret · Plan

3 · **Berre** · MARTIGUES · la Mède Ouest · la Mède-Est · **6** · Gignac · Pas-des-Lanciers · **27** · Cadeneaux · les Pennes · **17**

OUC · Mart.-Ferrières · Mart.-Lavera · la Jonquières · les Ventrons · **28** · Châteauneuf · les Marigues · Gignac-la-Nerthe · la Nerthe · Jas-de-Rhodes · la Gaotte · A55 · S.

Auguette · Pouteau · S.t Julien · la Bastide-Blanche · Carry-le-Rouet · Gignac-la-Nerthe · Douard · le Rove · St-André · Calade · **14**

les Rouets · S.te Croix · **Chaîne** · **17** · **de l'Estaque** · Ensuès-la-Redonne · **18** · la Vesse · Miolon · la Madrague-de-la-Ville · Les Parts

4 · la Couronne · Carro · Tamaris · Sausset-les-Pins · le Rouet-Plage · Madrague-de-Gignac · **Rade de Marseille** · **MARSEILLE** (Grec: Massilia)

Carré · Cap Couronne · Carry-le-Rouet · Île Ratonneau

C · **ô** · **t** · **e** · **B** · **l** · **e** · **u** · **e** · Château d'If · Île Pomègues · Île

5 · la Madrague-de-Montredon · Cap Croisette · Massif de Ma · **432** · les Goudes · Île Tiboulen · Île Maire · Île de Jarre

Île de Planier

6 · Wahrán (Oran) 25-27 h · Al Jazáir (Alger) 20 h · Bejaia 24 h · Skikda 24 h · Annaba 22 h · Tunis 22 h · Porto-Vecchio 13 h · Ajaccio 7-10 h · Propriano 8-11 h · l'Île-Rousse 8-11 h · Bastia 7-10 h · Île de

140

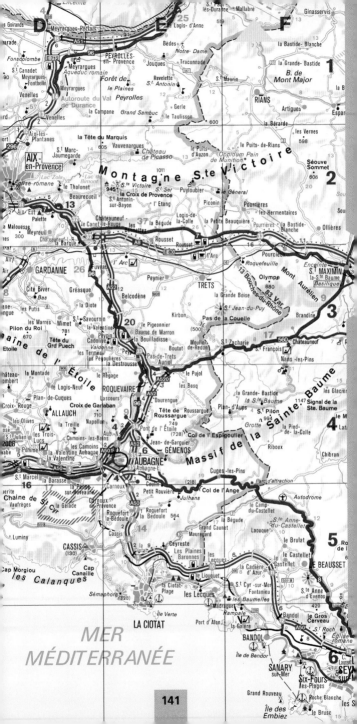

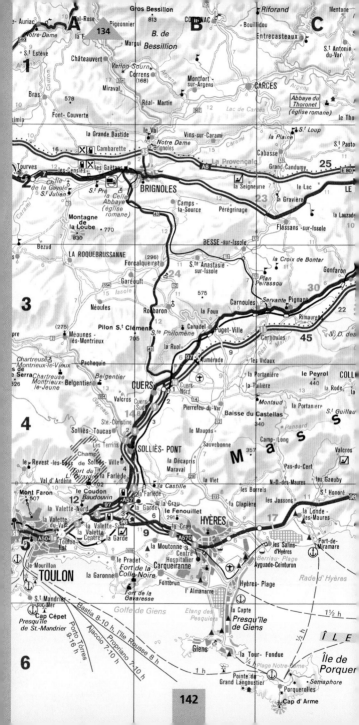

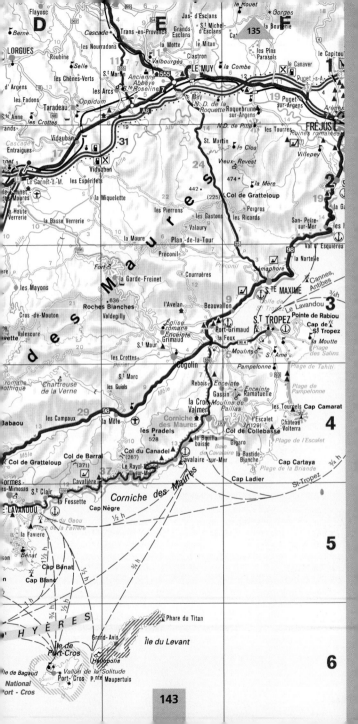

Sight Locator Index

This index relates to the atlas section on pages 130–143. We have given map references to the main sights of interest in the book. Some sights in the index may not be plotted on the atlas.

For the main index see pages 125–126